HEALTH CARE IN TRANSITION

HEALTH INSURANCE AFFORDABILITY AND THE ROLE OF PREMIUM TAX CREDITS

HEALTH CARE IN TRANSITION

Additional books in this series can be found on Nova's website under the Series tab.

Additional e-books in this series can be found on Nova's website under the e-book tab.

HEALTH CARE IN TRANSITION

HEALTH INSURANCE AFFORDABILITY AND THE ROLE OF PREMIUM TAX CREDITS

BRITTANY RODRIQUEZ
EDITOR

NOVINKA

New York

NOTICE TO THE READER

Additional color graphics may be available in the e-book version of this book.

Library of Congress Cataloging-in-Publication Data

ISBN: 978-1-63482-931-1

Published by Nova Science Publishers, Inc. † New York

CONTENTS

PREFACE

The number of uninsured individuals and the rising cost of health insurance have been long-standing issues. The Patient Protection and Affordable Care Act (PPACA) mandated that most individuals have health insurance that provides minimum essential coverage or pay a tax penalty. To make health insurance more affordable and expand access, PPACA created the advance premium tax credit (APTC) to subsidize the cost of exchange plans' premiums for those eligible. This book examines what is known about the effects of the APTC and the extent to which affordable health benefits plans are available and individuals are able to maintain minimum essential coverage. Furthermore, new federal tax credits, authorized under the PPCA, first became available in 2014 to help certain individuals pay for health insurance. The tax credits apply toward premiums for private health plans offered through exchanges (also referred to as health insurance marketplaces). This book provides examples of hypothetical individuals and families that qualify for the premium credits and describes the eligibility criteria applicable to the premium tax credits and cost-sharing subsidies, and the calculation method for the credit and subsidy amounts. It also highlights selected issues addressed in the final regulation and guidance on premium credits and indicates the status of implementation, where relevant data is available.

In: Health Insurance Affordability …
Editor: Brittany Rodriquez

ISBN: 978-1-63482-931-1

Chapter 1

PRIVATE HEALTH INSURANCE: EARLY EVIDENCE FINDS PREMIUM TAX CREDIT LIKELY CONTRIBUTED TO EXPANDED COVERAGE, BUT SOME LACK ACCESS TO AFFORDABLE PLANS*

United States Government Accountability Office

WHY GAO DID THIS STUDY

The number of uninsured individuals and the rising cost of health insurance have been long-standing issues. PPACA mandated that most individuals have health insurance that provides minimum essential coverage or pay a tax penalty. To make health insurance more affordable and expand access, PPACA created the APTC to subsidize the cost of exchange plans' premiums for those eligible. PPACA used two standards for defining affordability of health insurance: 8 percent of household income for the purposes of minimum essential coverage and 9.5 percent for APTC eligibility for individuals offered employer-sponsored plans.

* This is an edited, reformatted and augmented version of the United States Government Accountability Office publication, GAO-15-312, dated March 2015.

PPACA mandated that GAO review the affordability of health insurance coverage. GAO examined (1) what is known about the effects of the APTC and (2) the extent to which affordable health benefits plans are available and individuals are able to maintain minimum essential coverage. GAO conducted a structured literature search to identify studies on the rate of uninsured individuals, among other topics, and interviewed experts from HHS, the Internal Revenue Service (IRS), and 11 research and industry organizations to understand factors affecting affordability. GAO also analyzed the variation in the affordability of exchange plan premiums nationwide using 2014 data—the most recent data available at the time of GAO's analysis.

GAO received technical comments on a draft of this report from HHS and IRS and incorporated them as appropriate.

WHAT GAO FOUND

Early evidence suggests that the advance premium tax credit (APTC)—the refundable tax credit that can be paid on an advance basis—likely contributed to an expansion of health insurance coverage in 2014 because it significantly reduced the cost of exchange plans' premiums for those eligible. Although there are limitations to measuring the effects of the APTC using currently available data, surveys GAO identified estimated that the uninsured rate declined significantly among households with incomes eligible for the APTC. For example, one survey found that the rate of uninsured among individuals with household incomes that make them financially eligible for the APTC fell 5.2 percentage points between September 2013 and September 2014.This expansion in health insurance coverage is likely partially a result of the APTC having reduced the cost of health insurance premiums for those eligible. Among those eligible for the APTC who the Department of Health and Human Services (HHS) initially reported selected a plan through a federally facilitated exchange or one of two state-based exchanges, the APTC reduced premiums by 76 percent, on average. As of January 2015, data were not yet available on the extent to which the APTC reduced 2015 premiums, although studies have found that, on average, premiums (before applying the APTC) changed only modestly from 2014 to 2015, though some areas saw significant increases or decreases.

Most nonelderly adults had access to affordable health benefits plans—as defined by the Patient Protection and Affordable Care Act (PPACA)—but some may face challenges maintaining coverage. Most nonelderly adults had access to affordable plans through their employer, Medicaid, the exchanges, or other sources as of March 2014, although about 16 percent of nonelderly adults remained uninsured. While there are many reasons people remain uninsured, some people may not have access to affordable coverage, including (1) low- income nonelderly adults—those with household income below 100 percent of the federal poverty level—who live in one of the 23 states that chose not to expand Medicaid and (2) some nonelderly adults who do not have affordable employer-sponsored insurance and who were not eligible for the APTC. For those with incomes too high to qualify for the APTC, the affordability of health insurance coverage available in the individual exchanges in 2014 varied by age, household size, income, and location. For example, a 60-year-old with an income of 450 percent of the federal poverty level would have had to spend more than 8 percent of their household income for the lowest-cost plan in 84 percent of all health insurance rating areas in the United States, but a 27-year-old had access to an affordable plan in all but one. Regardless of the affordability of premiums, some may face challenges in maintaining coverage that qualifies under PPACA as minimum essential coverage; for example, changes in income can result in changes in APTC eligibility.

This report provides an early look at the effect of the APTC and the affordability of health insurance under PPACA. However, it is important to note that these findings about the first year of the exchanges cannot be generalized to future years. Numerous factors, including additional data and changes in trends in health care costs, could affect the affordability of health insurance going forward.

ABBREVIATIONS

AHRQ	Agency for Healthcare Research and Quality
APTC	Advance Premium Tax Credit
CBO	Congressional Budget Office
CMS	Centers for Medicare & Medicaid Services
ESI	employer-sponsored insurance
FPL	federal poverty level
HCERA	Health Care and Education Reconciliation Act of 2010
HHS	Department of Health and Human Services
IRS	Internal Revenue Service
KFF	The Henry J. Kaiser Family Foundation

MEPS	Medical Expenditure Panel Survey
PPACA	Patient Protection and Affordable Care Act
SHOP	Small Business Health Option Programs

* * *

March 23, 2015

Congressional Committees

The number of uninsured individuals and the rising cost of health insurance have been long-standing issues. From 1997 through 2013, the number of nonelderly uninsured in the United States fluctuated between about 30 and 42.5 million and was about 20.4 percent of the nonelderly population in 2013.[1] Many of these uninsured individuals were not eligible for public insurance, such as Medicaid—the joint federal-state health coverage program for certain low-income individuals—nor were they offered employer-sponsored insurance (ESI). Before 2014, their remaining option was to purchase a plan on the private, individual market, but these plans were often difficult to afford given that the uninsured typically have low incomes. In 2013, 85 percent of the uninsured were in households earning less than about 400 percent of the federal poverty level (FPL).[2]

The Patient Protection and Affordable Care Act (PPACA) included a number of provisions to address these challenges. Among other things, PPACA mandated that, with some exceptions, individuals must have health insurance that provides "minimum essential coverage" or pay a tax penalty, a requirement many refer to as the individual mandate.[3] Health insurance that meets the minimum essential coverage standard includes certain types of government-sponsored coverage (such as Medicare Part A or Medicaid) as well as most types of private insurance plans (such as ESI) that provide health benefits consistent with the law.[4]

To expand access to health insurance that qualifies as minimum essential coverage, PPACA created the premium tax credit to subsidize premium costs for plans purchased by eligible individuals and families through the exchanges—marketplaces where participating private issuers offer consumers a variety of qualified health plans that constitute minimum essential coverage.[5] Certain low- and moderate-income individuals and families may be eligible for this credit, which is refundable and can be paid to insurance companies in advance to reduce enrollees' premium costs for exchange plans. In this report, we refer to advance payments of the credit as advance premium tax credits (APTC).[6]

In addition, PPACA required the establishment of small business health option programs (SHOP) in each state to allow small employers to compare available health insurance options in their states and facilitate the enrollment of their employees in qualifying coverage. To provide an incentive for them to do so, PPACA established the small employer health insurance tax credit (referred to in this report as the small employer tax credit).[7] It subsidizes the share of the premiums small employers pay for their employees' health insurance. Individuals are exempt from the requirement to have minimum essential coverage when such coverage is not "affordable," as defined by PPACA. In general, plans are considered affordable if their cost does not exceed 8 percent of household income. In addition, for purposes of determining eligibility for the APTC, PPACA considers ESI affordable if an employee's share of a qualifying self-only plan costs no more than 9.5 percent of household income.[8] Individuals with an offer of ESI that meets or is below this threshold are not eligible to receive the APTC.

PPACA mandated that GAO review the affordability of health insurance coverage 5 years after enactment.[9] Specifically, in this report we examine

1. what is known about the effects of the APTC and the small employer tax credit on health insurance coverage; and
2. the extent to which affordable health benefits plans are available and individuals are able to maintain minimum essential coverage.

To examine what is known about the effects of the APTC and the small employer tax credit on health insurance coverage, we conducted a structured literature search to identify relevant studies.[10] To conduct this review, we searched over 30 reference databases for studies published on these topics. Two analysts independently reviewed each of the results for relevance. To supplement this search, we performed further Internet searches and asked experts we interviewed to recommend literature. We interviewed experts from 11 research or industry organizations as well as officials from the Department of Health and Human Services' (HHS) Center for Consumer Information and Insurance Oversight, Assistant Secretary of Planning and Evaluation, and the Chief Actuary; and from the Internal Revenue Service (IRS). We identified the experts through their published or other work, and we asked them about how the tax credits were likely to affect health insurance coverage. We also reviewed laws, regulations, and guidance related to PPACA's individual mandate, the APTC, the small employer tax credit, individual exchange regulation, and the ESI affordability threshold. To further analyze the effects of the small employer tax credit on health insurance coverage, we incorporated summary data from our previous report on this topic and requested updated summary data from the IRS on claims for tax years 2011 and 2012, the most current years available at the time of our analysis.[11] To assess the reliability of the data, we reviewed the data and supporting documentation for obvious errors, as well as IRS's internal controls for producing the data. We found the data to be sufficiently reliable for our purposes.

To examine the extent to which affordable health benefits plans are available and individuals are able to maintain minimum essential coverage, we reviewed studies resulting from our literature review, as well interviewed experts as described above. We asked experts about the types of individuals that may have more or less difficulty accessing affordable coverage and maintaining minimum essential coverage. In addition, we analyzed 2014 premium data—the most recent data available at the time of our analysis—from the federally facilitated exchanges and state-based exchanges to determine the percent of household income that households would have had to spend on premiums for the lowest-cost plans available. We obtained these premium data from The Henry J. Kaiser Family Foundation (KFF) and from the state of New York. To assess these data for reliability, we interviewed key officials, checked the data for outliers and validated selected data. We found both datasets to be reliable for our purposes. A more extensive discussion of our scope and methodology appears in appendix II.

We conducted this performance audit from July 2014 through March 2015 in accordance with generally accepted government auditing standards. Those standards require that we plan and perform the audit to obtain sufficient, appropriate evidence to provide a reasonable basis for our findings and conclusions based on our audit objectives. We believe that the evidence obtained provides a reasonable basis for our findings and conclusions based on our audit objectives.

BACKGROUND

PPACA Health Insurance Requirements and Subsidies

Beginning January 1, 2014, PPACA required most citizens and legal residents of the United States to maintain health insurance that qualifies as minimum essential coverage for themselves and their dependents or pay a tax penalty. Individuals are exempt from this requirement if they would have to pay more than 8 percent of their household income for the lowest-cost self-only health plan that is available to the individual.[12]

Beginning October 1, 2013, individuals were able to shop for private health insurance coverage that qualifies as minimum essential coverage through marketplaces, also referred to as exchanges, which offer choices of qualified health plans.[13] In 34 states, the federal government operated the individual exchanges, known as federally facilitated exchanges, while 17 states operated state-based exchanges in 2014.[14] Individuals can purchase self-only plans, or they can purchase family plans for themselves, their spouses, and their dependents.

Qualified health plans on the exchanges may provide minimum essential coverage at one of four levels of coverage that reflect out-of-pocket costs that may be incurred by an enrollee. The four levels of coverage correspond to a plan's actuarial value—the percentage of the total average costs of allowed benefits paid by a health plan—and are designated by metal tiers: 60 percent (bronze), 70 percent (silver), 80 percent (gold), and 90 percent (platinum).[15] For example, a gold plan with an 80 percent actuarial value would be expected to pay, on average, 80 percent of a standard population's expected medical expenses for the essential health benefits. The individuals covered by the plan would be expected to pay, on average, the remaining 20 percent of the expected cost-sharing expenses in the form of deductibles, copayments, and coinsurance.[16]

Under PPACA, issuers are allowed to adjust premium rates within specified limits for plans, based on the number of people covered under a particular policy and the covered individuals' age, tobacco use, and area of residence.[17] Each state must divide its state into one or more rating areas that all issuers must use in setting premium rates. The rating area is the lowest geographic level by which issuers can vary premiums.

Individuals obtaining insurance through the exchanges may be eligible for the APTC under PPACA if they meet applicable income requirements and are not be eligible for coverage under another qualifying plan or program, such as ESI or Medicaid. To meet the APTC's income requirements, individuals must have household incomes between 100 and 400 percent of the FPL (see table 1).[18]

Table 1. 2013 Federal Poverty Level (FPL) for an Individual and a Family of Four in the 48 Contiguous States

Percentage of Poverty	Poverty level for single person	Poverty level for family of four
100	$11,490	$23,550
133	$15,282	$31,322
200	$22,980	$47,100
300	$34,470	$70,650
400	$45,960	$94,200

Source: Department of Health and Human Services. | GAO-15-312

Note: The U.S. Department of Health and Human Services publishes separate FPL guidelines for Alaska and Hawaii that are higher than for the 48 continuous states, reflecting higher cost-of-living allowances.

The amount of the APTC is calculated based on an eligible individual's household income relative to the cost of premiums for the "reference plan," even if the individual chooses to enroll in a different plan. The reference plan is the second-lowest-cost silver plan available.[19] The APTC in effect caps the maximum amount of income that an individual would be required to contribute to the premiums for the reference plan. The capped amount varies depending on the enrollee's household income relative to the FPL and is less for enrollees with lower household income. Table 2 shows the maximum percentage of household income a qualifying enrollee would have to pay if they enrolled in the reference plan. If the enrollee chooses a more expensive plan, such as a gold or platinum plan, they would pay a higher percentage of their income. If the enrollee chooses a less expensive plan, such as a bronze plan, they would pay less.[20] The amount of the APTC is determined based on an enrollee's family size and anticipated household income for the year, which is subject to adjustment—or reconciliation—the following year. Specifically, the final amount of the credit is determined when the enrollee files an income tax return for the taxable year, which may result in a tax liability or refund if the enrollee's actual, reported household income amount is greater or less than the anticipated income on which the amount of APTC was based.

To further improve access to care, certain low-income individuals may also be eligible for an additional type of income-based subsidy established by PPACA, known as cost-sharing subsidies, which reduce out-of-pocket costs for such things as copayments for physician visits or prescription drugs.[21] To be eligible for these cost-sharing subsidies, individuals must have household incomes between 100 and 250 percent of the FPL, not be eligible for coverage under another qualifying plan or program such as Medicaid or ESI, and be enrolled in a silver plan through an exchange.[22] Cost-sharing subsidies effectively raise the actuarial value of the silver plan.

As a practical matter, because individuals eligible for Medicaid are not eligible for the APTC, the minimum income level for these subsidies differs between states that chose to expand Medicaid under PPACA and those that did not.[23] In states that chose to expand Medicaid under PPACA, nonelderly adults are eligible for Medicaid when their household income is less than 138 percent of the FPL. Because those eligible for Medicaid are not eligible for the APTC, the minimum income level for the APTC in Medicaid expansion states is effectively 138 percent of the FPL. In states that chose not to expand Medicaid, the minimum income level for individuals to qualify for APTC and cost-sharing subsidies is 100 percent of the FPL, as specified in PPACA, assuming the state's Medicaid eligibility threshold is at or below this level.[24] As of January 2015, 27 states and the District of Columbia opted to expand Medicaid under PPACA.

Table 2. Percentage of Household Income Enrollee Is Required to Contribute for Reference Plan Premiums, after Applying the APTC

Percentage of the FPL	Premium contribution as a percentage of income
0 to less than 100%	Generally does not qualify for APTC
At least 100 but less than 133%	2%
At least 133 but less than 150%	3-4%
At least 150 but less than 200%	4-6.3%
At least 200 but less than 250%	6.3-8.1%
At least 250 but less than 300%	8.1-9.5%
At least 301 but less than 400%	9.5%
Over 400%	Does not qualify for APTC

Source: IRS and 26 C.F.R. §§ 1.36B-2(b), 1.36B-3(g)(2) (2012). | GAO-15-312

Employer-Sponsored Insurance under PPACA

Under PPACA, employers that meet certain conditions must offer health insurance to some employees. Employers with at least 50 full-time equivalent employees—which includes employees whose hours average at least 30-hours per week—must offer qualifying health insurance to their full time employees or face tax penalties if at least one full-time employee receives the APTC.[25]

In contrast to PPACA's affordability threshold of 8 percent of household income for the purpose of assessing penalties for failure to maintain minimum essential coverage, PPACA requires ESI to meet two different affordability tests for the purposes of determining eligibility for the APTC. First, the employee's share of the ESI premiums covering an individual, also referred to as a self-only plan, must not exceed 9.5 percent of the employee's household income. Second, the insurance offered must cover 60 percent of the actuarial value of health care for the average person to qualify as affordable for purposes of the APTC. Employees who are offered ESI that meets both of these tests are not eligible for the APTC. Some employees may be offered qualifying ESI that costs between 8 and 9.5 percent of household income. If these individuals do not have access to insurance on an individual exchange that costs less than 8 percent of household income, they are exempt from the individual mandate and will not have to pay a tax penalty if they forgo coverage. However, these individuals are not eligible for the APTC.

Small Employer Tax Credit

Because small employers are not required to offer health insurance and have been less likely to offer health insurance than large employers, PPACA established a small employer tax credit as an incentive for them to provide insurance by making it more affordable.[26] The credit is available to certain employers—small business and tax-exempt entities— with employees earning low wages and that pay at least half of their employees' health insurance premiums. To qualify for the credit, employers must employ fewer than 25 full-time equivalent employees (excluding certain employees, such as business owners and their family members), and pay average annual wages per employee of less than $50,800 per year in 2014. The amount of the credit depends on several factors, such as the number of full-time equivalent employees and their total annual wages. In addition, the amount of the credit is limited if the premiums paid by an employer are more than the state's average small group market premiums, as determined by HHS.

Employers may claim the small employer tax credit for up to 6 years—the initial 4 years from 2010 through 2013 and, starting in 2014, any 2 consecutive years if they buy insurance through the Small Business Health Option Programs (SHOP). PPACA required the establishment of SHOPs in each state by January 1, 2014, to allow small employers to compare available health insurance options in their states and facilitate the enrollment of their employees in coverage. In states electing not to establish and operate a state-based SHOP, PPACA required the federal government to establish and operate a federally facilitated SHOP in the state.[27] Starting in 2014, employers that wanted to claim the small employer tax credit had to enroll their employees through the SHOP exchanges.

EARLY EVIDENCE SUGGESTS THAT WHILE THE APTC LIKELY CONTRIBUTED TO AN EXPANSION OF COVERAGE, THE SMALL EMPLOYER TAX CREDIT HAS HAD LITTLE EFFECT

Early evidence suggests that the APTC likely contributed to an expansion of health insurance coverage because it significantly reduced the cost of premiums for those eligible, though there are limitations to measuring the effects of the APTC using currently available data. In contrast, few employers claimed the small employer tax credit, limiting its effect on health insurance coverage.

The APTC Likely Contributed to an Expansion of Coverage by Reducing the Cost of Health Insurance Premiums to Those Eligible

Early evidence suggests that the APTC likely contributed to an expansion in health insurance coverage. We identified three surveys that estimated the uninsured rate by household income. Although limitations exist in measuring the direct, causal effects of the APTC on health insurance coverage using currently available data, these surveys can be used to make early observations about changes in the rate of uninsured. They found that the uninsured rate declined among households with incomes between 139 and 400 percent of the FPL—that is, households financially eligible for the APTC in all states (see table 3). For example, one study found that the rate of uninsured among individuals with household incomes between 139 and 400 percent of the FPL fell 9 percentage points between January 1, 2012, and June 30, 2014, in Medicaid expansion states.[28] Further, the results from this survey found that gains in insurance coverage were statistically significant for individuals in this income bracket regardless of the states' Medicaid expansion decisions.

Table 3. Survey Estimates of the Change in the Percent of Uninsured Nonelderly Adults by Household Income As a Percent of the Federal Poverty Level (FPL)

Survey	States covered	Time period	Income categories, as a percent of the FPL	Percentage point change in the rate of uninsured
Gallup-Healthways Well-Being Index[a]	Medicaid nonexpansion states	January 1, 2012, to June 30, 2014	Less than 139 percent of the FPL	-3.1
			139 to 400 percent of the FPL	-5.5
			Greater than 400 percent of the FPL	-1.0
	Medicaid expansion states	January 1, 2012, to June 30, 2014	Less than 139 percent of the FPL	-6.0
			139 to 400 percent of the FPL	-9.0
			Greater than 400 percent of the FPL	-0.7
The Commonwealth Fund Affordable Care Act Tracking Survey[b]	All states	July 15 to September 8, 2013, versus April 9 to June 2, 2014	Less than 138 percent of the FPL	-11.0
			138 to 249 percent of the FPL	-10.0
			250 to 399 percent of the FPL	-2.0

Survey	States covered	Time period	Income categories, as a percent of the FPL	Percentage point change in the rate of uninsured
			400 percent of the FPL or greater	-1.0
The Urban Institute Health Reform Monitoring Survey[c]	All states	September 2013 to September 2014	Less than 139 percent of the FPL	-12.0
			139 to 399 percent of the FPL	-5.2
			400 percent of the FPL or greater	-0.2

Source: GAO analysis. | GAO-15-312.

Notes: The three surveys cannot be compared directly because each survey covered different time periods, categorized respondents in slightly different income categories, and asked questions about individuals' health insurance coverage slightly differently.

[a] B. D. Sommers, T. Musco, K. Finegold, M. Z. Gunja, et al., "Health Reform and Changes in Health Insurance Coverage in 2014," *The New England Journal of Medicine*, vol. 371, no. 9 (2014).

[b] S. R. Collins, P. W. Rasmussen, and M. M. Doty. *Gaining Ground: Americans' Health Insurance Coverage and Access to Care after the Affordable Care Act's First Open Enrollment Period* (New York: The Commonwealth Fund, 2014).

[c] S. K. Long, M. Karpman, A. Shartzer, D. Wissoker, et al., *Taking Stock: Health Insurance Coverage under the ACA as of September 2014* (Washington, D.C.: The Urban Institute, 2014).

This expansion in health insurance coverage is likely partially a result of the APTC having reduced the cost of health insurance premiums for those deemed eligible.[29] As of April 19, 2014, HHS initially estimated that 8 million individuals (including dependents) had selected a health plan through either a state-based exchange or a federally facilitated exchange, and most of them (85 percent) were deemed eligible for the APTC at the time that they selected a health plan.[30] Among those who selected a plan through 1 of the 34 federally facilitated exchanges or the 2 state-based exchanges that used the federal website for enrollment in 2014 and were deemed eligible for the APTC (4.7 million individuals), the APTC reduced premiums by 76 percent, on average (see table 4).[31] For those who selected a silver plan through these 36 exchanges and were deemed eligible for the APTC, the APTC reduced premiums the most—an 80 percent reduction.[32] Overall, most individuals who selected a plan through these 36 exchanges and received the APTC (69 percent) saw their premiums reduced to $100 per month or less ($1,200 annually or less), and nearly half (46 percent) had their monthly premiums reduced to $50 or less ($600 annually or less).[33] However, results from an early survey and experts we interviewed suggested that the APTC may have been less effective in expanding health insurance coverage for individuals financially eligible for a smaller APTC amount and ineligible for cost- sharing reduction subsidies than for individuals eligible for a larger APTC amount as well as for cost-sharing reduction subsidies.[34]

Table 4. Average Monthly Advance Premium Tax Credit (APTC) Amount and Percent Reduction in Premiums after APTC for Individuals Who Selected a Plan through a Federally Facilitated Exchange or a State-Based Exchange that Used the Federal Website for Enrollment in 2014 and Were Deemed Eligible for the APTC in 2014, by Metal Tier

Metal tier	Average monthly premium amount before APTC	Average monthly APTC	Average monthly premium amount after APTC	Average percent reduction in premiums after APTC
Bronze	$289	$221	$68	76
Silver	$345	$276	$69	80
Gold	$428	$220	$208	51
Platinum	$452	$232	$220	51
All metal tiers	**$346**	**$264**	**$82**	**76**

Source: Department of Health and Human Services, Office of the Assistant Secretary for Planning and Evaluation, *Premium Affordability, Competition, and Choice in the Health Insurance Marketplace, 2014* (Washington, D.C.: June 18, 2014). | GAO-15-312

Notes: In its analysis of the amount of APTC that individuals received and the extent to which it reduced premiums, HHS included data from the 34 federally facilitated exchanges as well as 2 state- based exchanges—Idaho and New Mexico—that used the federal website, http://www.healthcare.gov, for exchange enrollment in 2014. Depending on the portion of health care costs expected to be paid by the health plan, qualified health plans are categorized into one of the following "metal tiers": bronze, silver, gold or platinum. Bronze plans cover an average of 60 percent of health care costs, silver plans cover 70 percent, gold plans cover 80 percent, and platinum plans cover 90 percent.

As of January 2015, data were not available on the extent to which the APTC reduced 2015 premiums for enrollees. Studies that examined changes in premiums between 2014 and 2015 found that, on average, premiums changed modestly. For example, HHS reported that premiums for the reference plan (before applying the APTC) increased by 2 percent, on average, between 2014 and 2015, and premiums for the lowest-cost silver plan increased by an average of 5 percent.[35] However, studies found variation across rating areas, and some rating areas had significant increases or decreases in average premiums.[36] Further, premiums are likely to continue to change in future years as issuers gain more data about enrollees in the exchanges and how they compare to enrollees previously purchasing individual insurance or ESI.[37] In addition, while the APTC helps protect eligible individuals from large increases in premiums by capping the amount of household income individuals have to pay for the reference plan, some who reenrolled in their health plan in 2015, rather than shopping for and switching to a lower cost plan, may find that their premiums, after accounting for the APTC, increased substantially. HHS estimated that more than 7 in 10 current exchange enrollees could find a lower-cost plan within the same metal level as they selected in 2014 if they selected the new lowest-cost plan in 2015, rather than reenroll in their same 2014 plan, but the extent to which this occurred was not yet known as of January 2015.[38]

According to results from four early surveys of nonelderly adults and one group of experts we interviewed, lack of awareness of the APTC may have limited take-up of health insurance coverage among some individuals likely eligible for the APTC. Three of the four surveys estimated that, of those who remained uninsured in 2014, between 59 and 60 percent cited affordability or the cost of premiums as the reason for not purchasing health insurance coverage.[39] However, less than half—between 38 and 47 percent—of the uninsured surveyed were aware of the availability of financial assistance to purchase insurance through the individual exchanges.[40]

When interpreting data on the effect of the APTC on changes in health insurance coverage, there are several limitations to consider:

- Large-scale, rigorous survey data are needed to more accurately measure the direct, causal effect of the APTC on changes in health insurance coverage. While early survey data provide some indications of the effect of the APTC on coverage, these surveys generally have lower response rates and smaller sample sizes, which could cause large margins of error when examining changes in health insurance coverage by subgroups, such as by household income.[41] However, results from larger, more rigorous surveys are not expected to be available until the summer of 2015 at the earliest.[42]

- Available summary data from HHS on those who received the APTC are limited and subject to change because the data:
  - Did not account for effectuated enrollment—that is, whether those who initially selected a health plan paid their premium—nor did it account for individuals who did not submit required documentation to verify their eligibility for the exchanges or the APTC, or those who may have selected a plan after open enrollment ended.[43]
  - Did not include the amount of APTC that individuals in 15 state-based exchanges received.[44] Although 15 state-based exchanges reported to HHS's Centers for Medicare & Medicaid Services (CMS) the number of individuals who were deemed eligible for the APTC at the time that they selected a plan, CMS officials we spoke with stated that voluntary reporting on the amount of APTC individuals received was limited and variable across states.
  - Did not account for adjustments to the amount of APTC that may occur when the amount of APTC received is reconciled against enrollees' actual income reported in their 2014 income tax returns, which will begin to occur when individuals start to file their income tax returns in 2015.[45]

Few Employers Claimed the Small Employer Tax Credit, Limiting Its Effect on Health Insurance Coverage

Take-up of the small employer tax credit has continued to be lower than anticipated, limiting the effect of the credit on expanding health insurance coverage. About 167,600 employers claimed the credit in 2012 (the most recent year for which data were available), slightly fewer than the 170,300 employers that claimed the credit in 2010 (see figure 1).[46] These figures are low compared to the number of employers eligible for the credit. In 2012, we found that selected estimates of the number of employers eligible ranged from about 1.4 million to 4 million.[47] Although about the same number of small employers claimed the credit in 2012 as in 2010, these employers paid all or some of the premiums for more employees in 2012 (900,800 employees) than in 2010 (770,000 employees).[48]

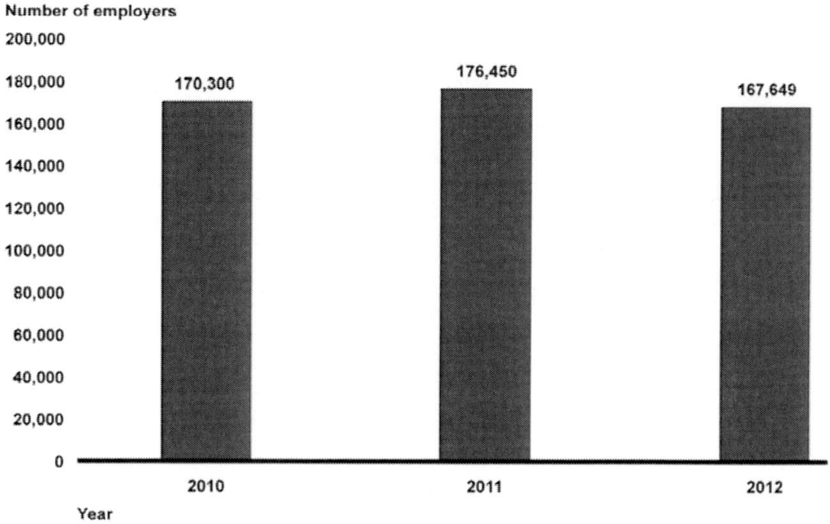

Source: IRS. | GAO-15-312.

Figure 1. Number of Employers That Claimed the Small Employer Tax Credit, 2010-2012.

As we found in 2012, experts we interviewed for this report generally told us that features of the small employer tax credit did not provide a strong enough incentive to employers to begin to offer or to continue offering health insurance.[49] First, experts explained that the maximum amount of the credit is targeted to very small employers, most of which do not offer health insurance, and experts told us the size of the credit is not large enough to be an incentive to employers to offer or maintain insurance. The maximum amount of the small employer tax credit is available to for- profit employers with ten or fewer full-time equivalent employees that pay an average of $25,400 or less in wages.[50] Such an employer could be eligible for a credit worth up to 50 percent of the employer contributions to premiums in 2014.[51] The credit amount "phases out" to zero as employers employ up to 25 full-time equivalent employees at higher wages—up to an average of $50,000. For example, employers with 24 full-time equivalent employees are only eligible for the credit if they paid wages that averaged $25,400 or less; such employers may be eligible for a credit worth up to 2.2 percent of employer contributions to premiums.[52] Second, the limited availability of the credit—employers can claim it for only two consecutive years after 2013—further detracts from any potential incentive for small employers that do not offer coverage to begin offering coverage. Experts we interviewed told us that employers are reluctant to provide a benefit to employees that would be at risk of being taken away later when the credit is no longer available.[53] Finally, experts told us that the complexity of applying for the credit outweighed its benefit. According to tax preparers and other stakeholders we interviewed for this and our previous report, the complexity of the paperwork required to claim the credit was significant, and small employers likely did not view the credit as a sufficient incentive to begin offering health insurance, given the time required to claim it.[54] The trend in low take-up of the small employer tax credit is likely to continue given the low enrollment in SHOPs, and thus it is unlikely that its effects on coverage will change in the near future. This is because employers were required to offer health insurance coverage through SHOP exchanges to be eligible for the small employer tax credit beginning in 2014.[55] We previously found that 2014 enrollment in SHOP was significantly below expectations. Specifically, we found that as of June 2014, the 18 state-based SHOP exchanges had enrolled about 76,000 employees through nearly 12,000 small employers,[56] although not all of these employers were eligible for the credit.[57] Enrollment in states with federally facilitated SHOPs was not known as of January 2015, although CMS officials said they did not have reason to expect significant differences in enrollment trends for 2014 between the state-based SHOPs and the federally facilitated SHOPs.[58] In comparison, the Congressional Budget Office (CBO) had estimated that, in 2014, 2 million employees would enroll in coverage through either state-based or federally facilitated SHOP exchanges.[59]

While Most Nonelderly Adults Had Access to Affordable Health Insurance Coverage, Maintaining Minimum Essential Coverage May Be Challenging for Some

Most nonelderly adults had access to affordable minimum essential coverage through their employer, Medicaid, the exchanges, or other sources, although about 16 percent of nonelderly adults remained uninsured as of March 2014. While there are many reasons people remain uninsured, some—including certain families or individuals not eligible for the APTC—may not have access to affordable coverage. The affordability of health insurance coverage obtained through the exchanges varied depending on one's age, household size, income, and place of residence. Regardless of the affordability of premiums, some may face challenges in maintaining their insurance.

Most Nonelderly Adults Had Access to Affordable Coverage

Most nonelderly adults had access to affordable minimum essential coverage through their employer, Medicaid, the exchanges, or other sources. While specific data on individuals' access to affordable coverage is not available, estimates of the number of nonelderly adults who are insured through various types of coverage indicate that most have access to coverage that would be considered affordable under PPACA. For example, one survey estimated that, as of March 2014, 59 percent of nonelderly adults had obtained coverage through an employer.[60] For most individuals with ESI, the coverage would be considered affordable under PPACA—that is, premiums for the self-only ESI plan offered cost less than 9.5 percent of their household income.[61] Individuals who are offered ESI that does not meet this affordability threshold may be eligible, depending on their household income, to receive the APTC to instead purchase an affordable exchange plan.[62] As of March 2014, an estimated 2 percent of nonelderly adults purchased coverage through an exchange—an estimated 85 percent of whom received the APTC. An additional 9 percent of nonelderly adults were enrolled in Medicaid coverage, which requires either no or minimal premiums.[63] Finally, an estimated 14 percent of nonelderly adults had other sources of coverage, such as TRICARE for certain members of the armed forces, or health plans sold off the exchanges.[64]

Some Groups of Nonelderly Adults May Lack Access to Affordable Health Insurance Coverage

An estimated 16 percent of nonelderly adults (31.4 million) were uninsured as of March 2014, according to one early survey.[65] CBO estimated that, in 2016, most of those who will remain uninsured—at least 77 percent—will likely be exempt from the requirement to maintain minimum essential coverage because, for example, they are undocumented immigrants or lack access to health insurance coverage that is considered affordable under PPACA.[66] While there are many reasons people remain uninsured, some individuals may not have access to affordable health insurance coverage.[67] For example, some may be low-income and live in a Medicaid nonexpansion state or they may lack access to affordable ESI yet are also ineligible for the APTC to instead purchase affordable coverage through the individual exchanges.

Low-Income Individuals Living in Medicaid Nonexpansion States

Nonelderly adults with household incomes less than 100 percent of the FPL are not eligible for the APTC and, if their state chose not to expand Medicaid to low-income adults, they may not be eligible for Medicaid.[68] Without financial assistance from an APTC, coverage available through the individual exchanges was likely unaffordable for these uninsured individuals. For example, an individual age 27 with household income at 99 percent of the FPL in a Medicaid nonexpansion state would have had to spend between 10 and 32 percent of their household income on the lowest-cost bronze plan, depending on their place of residence.[69] One study estimated that roughly 4 million nonelderly adults with household incomes below 100 percent of the FPL living in a Medicaid nonexpansion state were uninsured in 2014.[70]

Some Families with ESI

Although some families have access to ESI that is considered affordable under PPACA, they may have to spend more than 9.5 percent of their household income on such coverage. The ESI affordability threshold is based on the cost of a self-only plan even though premiums for a family plan are typically more expensive, requiring them to spend more than they would on a self-only plan. Because the family would be considered to have access to affordable ESI under PPACA based on the self-only plan, it would not be eligible to receive financial assistance through the APTC to purchase a family plan through the individual exchanges. This has created a situation that some have referred to as "the family glitch," where families offered ESI may find that coverage to be unaffordable yet they are ineligible for the APTC. The Agency for Healthcare Research and Quality (AHRQ) recently estimated that 10.5 million adults and children may be in this situation.[71]

Some Individuals without Affordable ESI Who Are Not Financially Eligible for the APTC

Some nonelderly adults who lack access to affordable coverage elsewhere, such as through an employer, and instead shop for health insurance coverage on the individual exchanges may find this insurance unaffordable without financial assistance from the APTC—those with household incomes greater than 400 percent of the FPL.[72] Results from one early survey suggest that about 6 percent of nonelderly adults were uninsured in 2014 and had household income greater than 400 percent of the FPL.[73] In addition, based on nine household scenarios we examined, the affordability of the lowest-cost bronze plans available in the individual exchanges for such individuals varied by age, household size, income, and location in 2014.[74] For example, in most rating areas in 2014 the lowest-cost bronze plan available would have been considered unaffordable to older individuals with household income between, for example, 401 and 500 percent of the FPL. However, in nearly all rating areas such coverage was likely affordable for younger individuals regardless of their household income.[75] The affordability of the lowest-cost bronze plans also varied by location and income for a family of four with two parents aged 40 years old and two children under 21 years of age. (See figure 2. For a more detailed version of the maps included in fig. 2, see appendix III.)

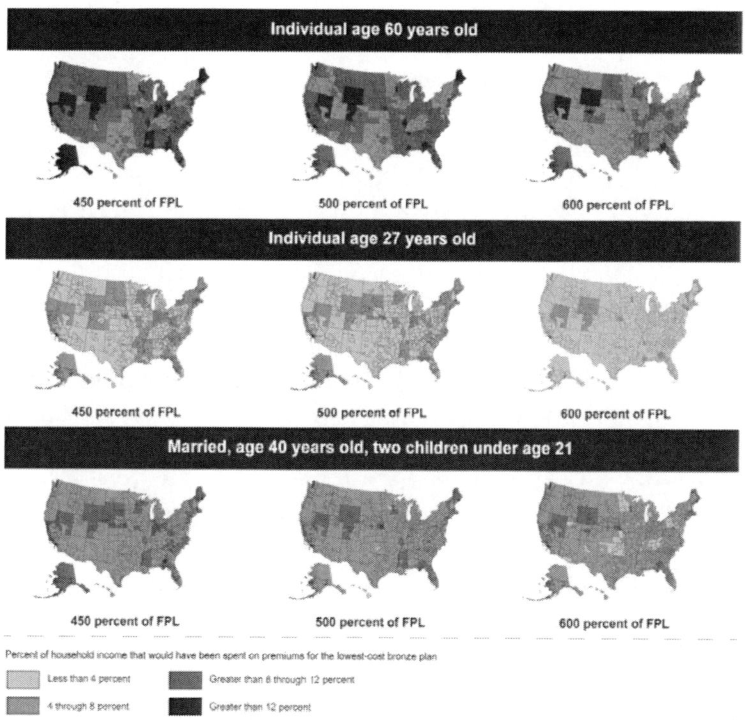

Source: GAO analysis of The Henry J. Kaiser Family Foundation data and New York state individual exchange data (data); Map Resources (map). | GAO 15-312

Note: Depending on the portion of health care costs expected to be paid by the health plan, qualified health plans are categorized into one of the following "metal tiers": bronze, silver, gold or platinum. Bronze plans cover an average of 60 percent of health care costs, silver plans cover 70 percent, gold plans cover 80 percent, and platinum plans cover 90 percent. The boundary lines in each of the maps depict the rating areas within each state except for Alaska. In Alaska, the boundary lines depict the three-digit zip codes in the state. In addition, due to how two zip codes are defined in Idaho, there are two areas in the state that were not assigned to a rating area and thus were left blank.

Figure 2. Percentage of Household Income That Would Have to Be Spent on Premiums for the Lowest-Cost Bronze Plan by Household Characteristics and Income As a Percent of the Federal Poverty Level (FPL) (2014).

Based on nine household scenarios we examined, the affordability of the lowest-cost bronze plans available varied across different demographic subsets in the United States, for example:

- **Individual age 60-years-old:** A 60-year-old individual with household income at 450 percent of the FPL would have had to spend greater than 8 percent of their household income for the lowest-cost bronze plan in most (84 percent) of the 501 rating areas in the United States.[76] Specifically, in 17 percent of rating areas such an individual would have had to spend greater than 12 percent of their household income, in nearly two-thirds (67 percent) of rating areas they would have had to spend greater than 8 through 12 percent, and in 16 percent of all rating areas they would have had to spend from 4 through 8 percent of their household income on the lowest-cost bronze plan.[77] Even with somewhat higher household income at 500 percent of the FPL, the lowest-cost bronze plan would be considered unaffordable for older individuals in most rating areas (72 percent). Moreover, in the most expensive rating area for a 60-year-old individual (counties near Albany, GA), the lowest-cost bronze plan had an annual premium of $9,487. Among those with income too high to receive the APTC, this plan would have been considered unaffordable for a 60-year-old individual if they earned between $46,797 (401 percent of the FPL) and $118,588 (1,016 percent of the FPL) in that rating area.[78]
- **Individual age 27-years-old:** The lowest-cost bronze plan would have been considered affordable in all but one rating area for a 27-

year-old with income too high to receive the APTC. In nearly half (47 percent) of all rating areas, such individuals with household income at 450 percent of the FPL, for example, would have had to spend from 4 through 8 percent of their income on the lowest-cost bronze plan, and in 53 percent of rating areas they would have had to spend less than 4 percent of their income. There is only one rating area where 27-year-olds with household income greater than 400 percent of the FPL would have had to spend greater than 8 percent of their household income on the lowest-cost bronze plan. In the most expensive rating area for a 27-year-old (the state of Vermont), the lowest-cost bronze plan had an annual premium of $4,032. Among those with income too high to receive the APTC, this plan would have been considered unaffordable for a 27-year-old individual if they earned between $46,797 (401 percent of the FPL) and $50,400 (432 percent of the FPL) in that rating area.[79]

- **Married couple age 40-years-old with two children under 21-years-old:** In 75 percent of all rating areas such a family with household income at 450 percent of the FPL would have had to spend from 4 through 8 percent of its household income on the lowest-cost bronze plan, and in 25 percent of all rating areas it would have had to spend greater than 8 through 12 percent of its household income. In one rating area such a family would have had to spend greater than 12 percent of its household income. In the most expensive rating area for a married couple aged 40 with two children and household income too high to receive the APTC (counties near Albany, GA), the lowest-cost bronze plan had an annual premium of $13,374, which would have been considered unaffordable for such a family if it earned between $95,639 (401 percent of the FPL) and $167,176 (701 percent of the FPL) in that rating area.[80]

Changes in premiums for plans offered on the individual exchanges between 2014 and 2015 likely affected variation in the affordability of lowest-cost bronze plans by rating area in 2015. Studies have estimated that, while the average cost of premiums for the reference or lowest-cost plans have changed only modestly between 2014 and 2015, average premiums increased significantly in some rating areas and decreased significantly in others.

Even Those with Affordable Premiums Could Face Challenges Maintaining Minimum Essential Insurance Coverage and Paying for High Out-of-Pocket Costs

Regardless of the affordability of premiums, some may face challenges in maintaining minimum essential coverage, and for those who retain insurance, obtaining health care may be costly. For example, among those eligible for the APTC, some may experience changes in their income that affect their eligibility, which may lead to coverage gaps or discontinuity in coverage.[81] It is too soon to know how many people became ineligible for the APTC in 2014, but experts we interviewed and studies of past years' data indicate that income changes are fairly common, particularly among those with lower incomes.[82] Changes in employment status and family composition can change enrollees' eligibility for certain types of insurance, which could lead to challenges maintaining health insurance. For example, a change in employment status can affect eligibility for ESI, the most common form of insurance for the nonelderly. One survey found that among nonelderly adults who reported having had a gap in ESI coverage in 2011, 67 percent reported that it was due to a change in employment status.[83] Changes in family composition can also cause challenges for people seeking to maintain health insurance. For example, divorce can cause one spouse to lose access to the other's ESI, or may change household income such that eligibility changes for federal subsidies or Medicaid.

Even if individuals are able to maintain health insurance that meets the criteria for minimum essential coverage, obtaining medical care may be costly. When enrollees receive health care services, they are often responsible for cost-sharing payments such as copayments or coinsurance. Enrollees' cost-sharing responsibilities for silver, gold, and platinum plans are lower than for bronze plans, but out-of-pocket costs for all plans can be considerable depending on an enrollee's health care needs and the structure of one's health plan. Insurers can structure plans to charge more or less for certain services or medications, as long as the out-of-pocket costs are limited to no more than $6,350 per year for in- network goods and services for single coverage of those with incomes above 250 percent of FPL.[84] For an enrollee with income of 251 percent of FPL ($28,725), $6,350 represents about 22 percent of their annual income.[85] Experts we interviewed stated that all exchange enrollees are vulnerable to high out-of-pocket costs, particularly if they seek care from out-of- network health care providers. Costs incurred by using out-of-network providers do not count toward a plan's out-of-pocket maximum, are not required to contribute toward a plan's deductible, and are ineligible for federal cost-sharing subsidies. Furthermore, experts told us that some insurers have limited the networks of providers covered by the plans offered on the exchanges. Experts explained that restricting networks allows insurers to reduce premiums by limiting the number of provider choices, but increases the possibility that a provider sought by an enrollee will be out-of-network.

CONCLUDING OBSERVATIONS

This report provides an early look at the effect of the tax credits and affordability of health insurance under PPACA, finding that evidence suggests that the APTC likely contributed to an expansion of health insurance coverage because it significantly reduced the cost of premiums for those eligible. However, the effects of the APTC and the affordability of health insurance in 2014 and beyond is uncertain for several reasons. First, complete data on the number of people who claimed the APTC in 2014 and the amount of the APTC claimed are not yet available because of the limited data reported from most state-based exchanges as well as the lag time during which enrollees file taxes and IRS completes reconciliation. Second, insurers will likely adjust premiums in exchange plans as more data become available about enrollees in the exchanges, including how the health profiles of exchange enrollees compares to that of enrollees previously purchasing individual insurance or ESI. Thus, trends for premiums in exchange plans may not stabilize for several years, although PPACA established certain requirements intended to reduce variation. Third, health insurance premiums are in large part driven by the underlying costs of health care. While the rate of growth of health care costs has slowed in recent years, there is no guarantee that such a trend will continue. As a result, it is important to note that our findings about the first year of the exchanges cannot be generalized to future years.

AGENCY COMMENTS

We received technical comments on a draft of this report from HHS and IRS and incorporated them as appropriate.

John E. Dicken, Director, Health Care

Appendix I: Potential Effects of Changing the Affordability Threshold for Employer-Sponsored Insurance

In addition to the two objectives we addressed in this report, PPACA mandated that GAO review what is known about the potential effects of lowering the employer-sponsored insurance (ESI) affordability threshold.[86] Under the 2014 income threshold, "affordable" means that employees' premium contribution for a self-only plan must cost no more than 9.5 percent of their household income.

Our literature review found no peer-reviewed studies that have examined the effects of lowering the ESI affordability threshold below 9.5 percent of household income.[87] However, experts to whom we spoke described mixed potential effects. Lowering the ESI affordability threshold would shift more of the cost of premiums onto employers—that is, employers would have to increase their contribution towards employees' premiums. Some experts stated that such a shift could encourage some employers to discontinue offering health insurance. In particular, experts told us that employers most likely to discontinue are those that employ a low-wage workforce. These employers face less competition in attracting lower-paid workers than higher-paid workers, so they have less incentive to offer health insurance coverage to attract workers. Employers with more than 50 full-time equivalent employees that do not provide health insurance coverage would be subject to the tax penalty on employers if any of their employees obtain health insurance coverage through the exchanges with assistance from the advance premium tax credit (APTC).[88] One expert commented that employers that cease offering health insurance may also choose to compensate employees for the loss of health insurance by increasing wages. Alternatively, one expert told us that employers that choose to continue offering health insurance might adjust employees' compensation packages to account for an increase in the employer contribution to health insurance premiums. These employers would avoid the tax penalty on employers that fail to offer affordable health insurance to employees.

Experts to whom we spoke stated that if the threshold were lowered, overall, federal costs would likely increase, although the magnitude of such an increase is unclear. Federal costs would increase if employers stop offering health insurance and employees that subsequently seek exchange coverage are eligible for and claim the APTC and cost-sharing subsidies. At the same time, federal tax revenue may also increase if employers dropping health insurance raised taxable wages and paid employer penalties because of their failure to offer health insurance. However, experts told us this increase in tax revenue would likely not be high enough to offset the increase in federal costs from employees' APTC and cost-sharing subsidy claims.

Because studies have estimated that relatively few people have an offer from their employer of self-only health insurance coverage that exceeds the affordability threshold of 9.5 percent of household income, relatively few are likely to be affected if the threshold were lowered. Three studies varied in their estimates, with the highest estimating up to 1 million people may have such an offer.[89] In comparison, the Congressional Budget Office (CBO) estimates that in 2014, 156 million nonelderly people received ESI coverage. The three studies found:

- The Agency for Healthcare Research and Quality (AHRQ) estimated that about one million people with household incomes between 139 to 400 percent of the federal poverty level (FPL) have an unaffordable offer.[90]
- CBO estimated that between 0 and 500,000 people had an unaffordable offer in 2014 and sought coverage on an exchange.[91]
- Another study combined different data sets to generate estimates of the number of households that had an unaffordable ESI offer.[92] The study found that if employers keep employee contributions at the national average (which the study authors calculated as 20 percent for self-only coverage in 2009), no employees' contribution would have exceeded the ESI affordability threshold in 2009.

These studies estimated that a relatively low number of people are offered ESI coverage that exceed 9.5 percent of their income because generally, employee contributions for self-only ESI coverage are small compared to income.

The average ESI premiums in 2014 were $6,025 per year for single coverage, and employees contributed about $1,081, on average.[93] Employees with household income of more than $11,380 would be considered to have affordable premiums.

APPENDIX II. OBJECTIVES, SCOPE AND METHODOLOGY

To describe what is known about the effects of the Advance Premium Tax Credit (APTC) and the small employer tax credit on health insurance coverage, as well as what is known about the potential effects of changing the employer-sponsored insurance (ESI) affordability threshold, we conducted a structured literature search for studies. To conduct this review, we searched over 30 bibliographic databases, including ABI/INFORM Global, MEDLINE, and WorldCat, for studies on these topics published between January 1, 2010, and November 12, 2014. Two analysts independently reviewed each of the results for relevance and then reconciled differences. We determined that a study was directly relevant to our objectives if it: (1) included empirical analysis related to the effects of the APTC or the small employer tax credit on the provision of health insurance or maintenance of health insurance; or (2) analyzed the effects of changing the ESI affordability threshold on the actions of employers, employees, or the federal budget. To supplement our search of reference databases, we:

- searched the Internet using Google.com and terms such as "APTC maintain health insurance" and "surveys insurance Patient Protection and Affordable Care Act (PPACA)";
- searched the websites of health policy research organizations such as the Henry J. Kaiser Family Foundation (KFF), the Urban Institute, and the American Enterprise Institute; and
- asked the experts we interviewed to recommend sources of literature that would address our objectives.

Through all of these literature searches, we identified 23 studies that were useful for the objectives of our report.[94] Among these studies, we identified summary results from three surveys that estimated the change in the rate of uninsured nonelderly adults between 2013 and 2014 by household income amounts comparable to APTC eligibility limits.[95] These surveys generally had low response rates and small sample sizes, which can introduce potential errors in estimating individuals' health insurance status, especially by population subgroups, such as by individuals' household income or type of health insurance coverage. Table 5 provides a summary of the response rate, sample size, and margin of error for these three surveys. To improve the reliability of estimates produced from the survey results, the studies' authors used certain sampling methodologies, such as stratified sampling to over-sample populations commonly underrepresented in such surveys (e.g., low-income populations), and weighted regression models. In addition, the authors validated their estimates against prior estimates from larger, more rigorous surveys, such as the American Community Survey, and found their estimates to be generally comparable, though with small differences in some cases. Because of these approaches to improve reliability, we determined the studies were sufficiently reliable for our purposes.

We also reviewed laws, regulations, and guidance related to PPACA's individual mandate, the APTC, the small employer tax credit, individual exchange regulation, and the ESI affordability threshold. We also reviewed the legislative history of the ESI affordability threshold.

We interviewed a range of experts to explore what is known about the effects of the APTC and the small employer tax credit on health insurance coverage and what is known about the extent to which health benefit plans are available and individuals are able to maintain minimum essential coverage, as well as what is known about the potential effects of changing the ESI affordability threshold. We asked experts at 11 research and industry organizations, in addition to officials at the Department of Health and Human Services (HHS) and the Internal Revenue Service (IRS), about their work related to the potential effect of tax credits on health insurance coverage, the types of individuals that may have more or less difficulty maintaining minimum essential coverage, and the potential effects on employers, employees, and federal costs of changing the ESI affordability threshold (we did not ask every question of every expert). We chose these experts based on relevance of their published or other work to our objectives.[96]

To further analyze what is known about the effects of the small employer tax credit on health insurance coverage, we requested summary data from the IRS on small employer tax credit claims, the number of employee premiums covered, and the total cost of the credit that IRS provided for tax years 2011 and 2012. Data on tax year 2013 and 2014 were not available at the time of our analysis. To assess the reliability of the data, we reviewed the data and supporting documentation for obvious errors, as well as IRS's internal controls for producing the data.[97] We found the data to be sufficiently reliable for our purposes. To supplement these data, we also incorporated summary data from our previous report on this topic.[98]

To describe the extent to which affordable health benefits plans are available and individuals are able to maintain minimum essential coverage, we analyzed 2014 premium data—the most recent data available at the time of our analysis—for health benefit plans offered through the exchanges. We obtained data from two sources. First, The Henry J. Kaiser Family Foundation (KFF) provided us with data on premiums for all health plans offered in the individual health insurance exchanges by rating area, excluding New York. KFF compiled the data using HHS's Centers for Medicare & Medicaid Services' Landscape file, which, for 2014, captured data on premiums for plans participating in the 34 federally facilitated exchanges and 2 state-based exchanges that used the federal website, http://www.healthcare.gov, for enrollment.[99] KFF supplemented the Landscape file data with data on premiums for plans offered in the other 15 state-based exchanges, which it acquired by reviewing health insurance companies' rate filings in each state and validating these data through state exchange websites when possible. We assessed the reliability of these data by: interviewing KFF officials about how they compiled and validated the data as well as their internal controls, testing the data for duplicate data and outliers, and comparing the publicly available Landscape data on federally facilitated exchanges to the KFF data. Second, from the state of New York, we obtained premium data for plans offered through the state's individual exchange during the initial open enrollment period (October 1, 2013, through March 31, 2014). To assess these data for reliability, we checked the data for outliers and validated selected data through the New York state exchange website. We found both the KFF data and the New York data to be sufficiently reliable for our purposes.

Using the data from these sources, we calculated the percent of household income that nine hypothetical individuals or households would have had to spend on premiums for the lowest cost bronze plans in each rating area in the United States in 2014, assuming different levels of household income as a percentage of the federal poverty level.[100] We also calculated the amount of household income that each hypothetical individual or household would need in order to pay 8 percent of household income for the lowest-cost bronze plan available by rating area.

We conducted this performance audit from July 2014 through March 2015 in accordance with generally accepted government auditing standards. Those standards require that we plan and perform the audit to obtain sufficient, appropriate evidence to provide a reasonable basis for our findings and conclusions based on our audit objectives. We believe that the evidence obtained provides a reasonable basis for our findings and conclusions based on our audit objectives.

Table 5. Methodological Information for Surveys That Estimated the Change in the Rate of Uninsured Nonelderly Adults

Survey	Time period surveyed	Survey response rate	Sample size	Sampling error (at 95 percent confidence interval)[a]
Gallup Healthways Well-Being Index	January 2012 to June 2014	11%	420,449	+/-1.0
The Commonwealth Fund Affordable Care Act Tracking Survey	July 15 to September 8, 2013 and April 9 to June 2, 2014	14%	4,425	+/- 2.1
The Urban Institute Health Reform Monitoring Survey	September 2013 to September 2014	5%	7,500b	+/-1.3

Source: GAO analysis. | GAO-15-312

Notes:

[a] Sampling error is the extent to which the survey results differ from what would have been obtained if the whole population had been observed.

[b] The Urban Institute's Health Reform Monitoring Survey (HRMS) samples approximately 7,500 nonelderly adults each quarter. HRMS data from the third quarter of 2013 and the third quarter of 2014 were used to estimate changes in the rate of uninsured nonelderly adults between September 2013 through September 2014.

APPENDIX III: AFFORDABILITY OF THE LOWEST-COST BRONZE PLAN, BY RATING AREA

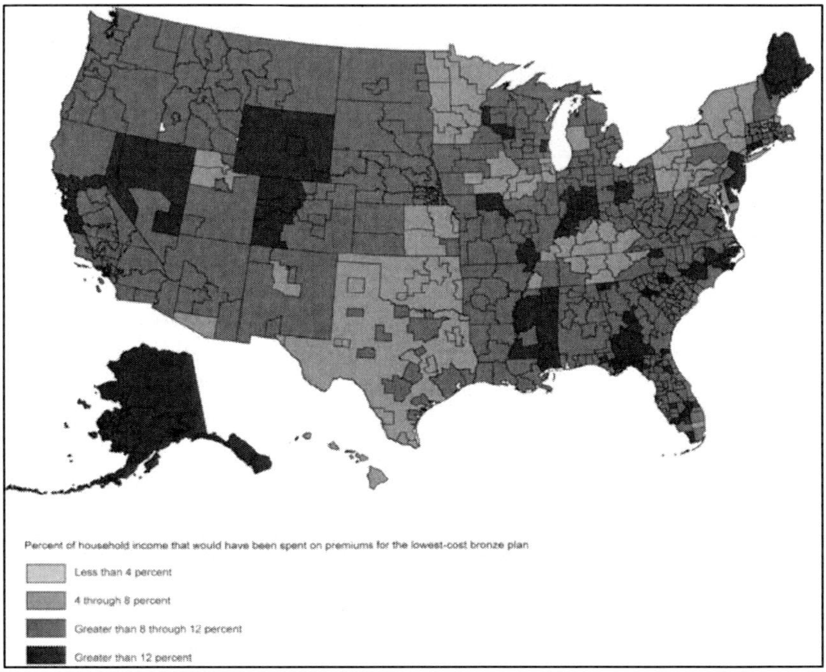

Source: GAO analysis of The Henry J. Kaiser Family Foundation data and New York state individual exchange data (data); Map Resources (map). | GAO 15-312

Note: Depending on the portion of health care costs expected to be paid by the health plan, qualified health plans are categorized into one of the following "metal tiers": bronze, silver, gold or platinum. Bronze plans cover an average of 60 percent of health care costs, silver plans cover 70 percent, gold plans cover 80 percent, and platinum plans cover 90 percent. The boundary lines depict the rating areas within each state except for Alaska. In Alaska, the boundary lines depict the three-digit zip codes in the state. In addition, due to how two zip codes are defined in Idaho, there are two areas in the state that were not assigned to a rating area and thus were left blank.

Figure 3. Percentage of Household Income That Would Have to Be Spent on Premiums for the Lowest-Cost Bronze Plan for a 60-Year-Old Individual with Household Income at 450 Percent of the Federal Poverty Level (2014).

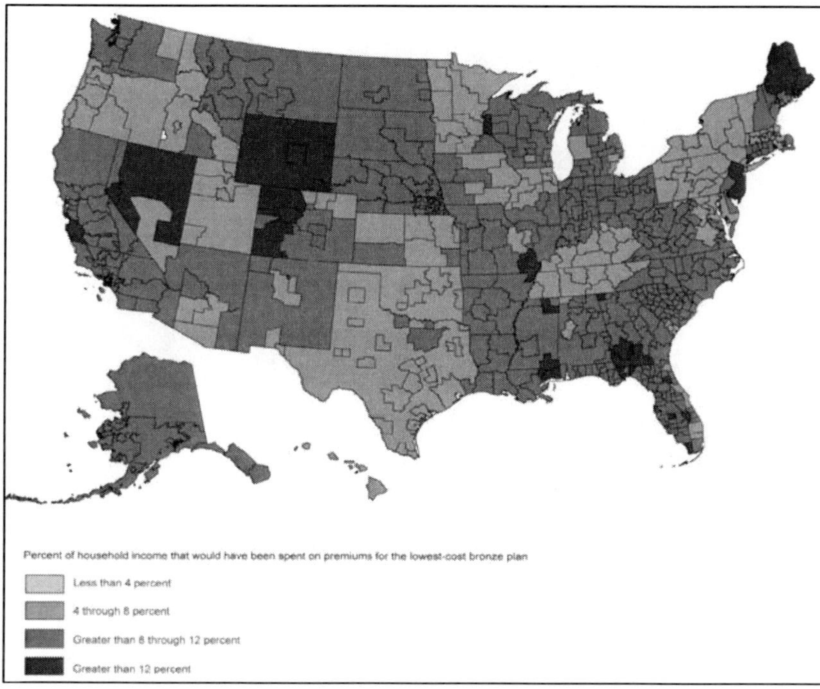

Source: GAO analysis of The Henry J. Kaiser Family Foundation data and New York state individual exchange data (data); Map Resources (map). | GAO 15-312

Note: Depending on the portion of health care costs expected to be paid by the health plan, qualified health plans are categorized into one of the following "metal tiers": bronze, silver, gold or platinum. Bronze plans cover an average of 60 percent of health care costs, silver plans cover 70 percent, gold plans cover 80 percent, and platinum plans cover 90 percent. The boundary lines depict the rating areas within each state except for Alaska. In Alaska, the boundary lines depict the three-digit zip codes in the state. In addition, due to how two zip codes are defined in Idaho, there are two areas in the state that were not assigned to a rating area and thus were left blank.

Figure 4. Percentage of Household Income That Would Have to Be Spent on Premiums for the Lowest-Cost Bronze Plan for a 60-Year-Old Individual with Household Income at 500 Percent of the Federal Poverty Level (2014).

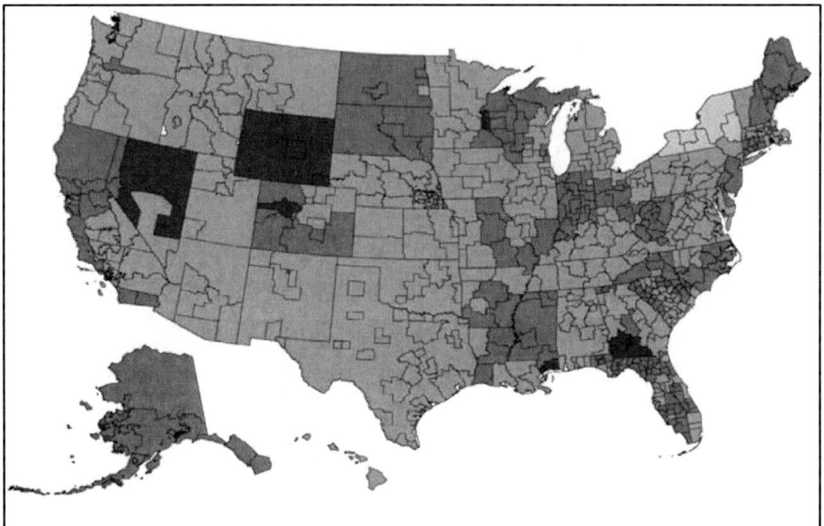

Source: GAO analysis of The Henry J. Kaiser Family Foundation data and New York state individual exchange data (data); Map Resources (map). | GAO 15-312

Note: Depending on the portion of health care costs expected to be paid by the health plan, qualified health plans are categorized into one of the following "metal tiers": bronze, silver, gold or platinum. Bronze plans cover an average of 60 percent of health care costs, silver plans cover 70 percent, gold plans cover 80 percent, and platinum plans cover 90 percent. The boundary lines depict the rating areas within each state except for Alaska. In Alaska, the boundary lines depict the three-digit zip codes in the state. In addition, due to how two zip codes are defined in Idaho, there are two areas in the state that were not assigned to a rating area and thus were left blank.

Figure 5. Percentage of Household Income That Would Have to Be Spent on Premiums for the Lowest-Cost Bronze Plan for a 60-Year-Old Individual with Household Income at 600 Percent of the Federal Poverty Level (2014).

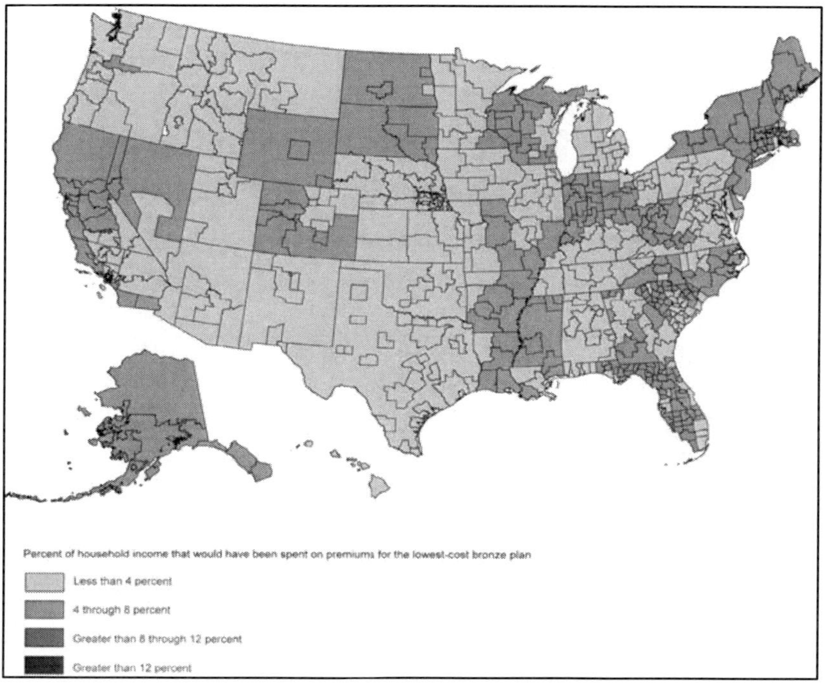

Source: GAO analysis of The Henry J. Kaiser Family Foundation data and New York state individual exchange data (data); Map Resources (map). | GAO 15-312

Note: Depending on the portion of health care costs expected to be paid by the health plan, qualified health plans are categorized into one of the following "metal tiers": bronze, silver, gold or platinum. Bronze plans cover an average of 60 percent of health care costs, silver plans cover 70 percent, gold plans cover 80 percent, and platinum plans cover 90 percent. The boundary lines depict the rating areas within each state except for Alaska. In Alaska, the boundary lines depict the three-digit zip codes in the state. In addition, due to how two zip codes are defined in Idaho, there are two areas in the state that were not assigned to a rating area and thus were left blank.

Figure 6. Percentage of Household Income That Would Have to Be Spent on Premiums for the Lowest-Cost Bronze Plan for a 27-Year-Old Individual with Household Income at 450 Percent of the Federal Poverty Level (2014).

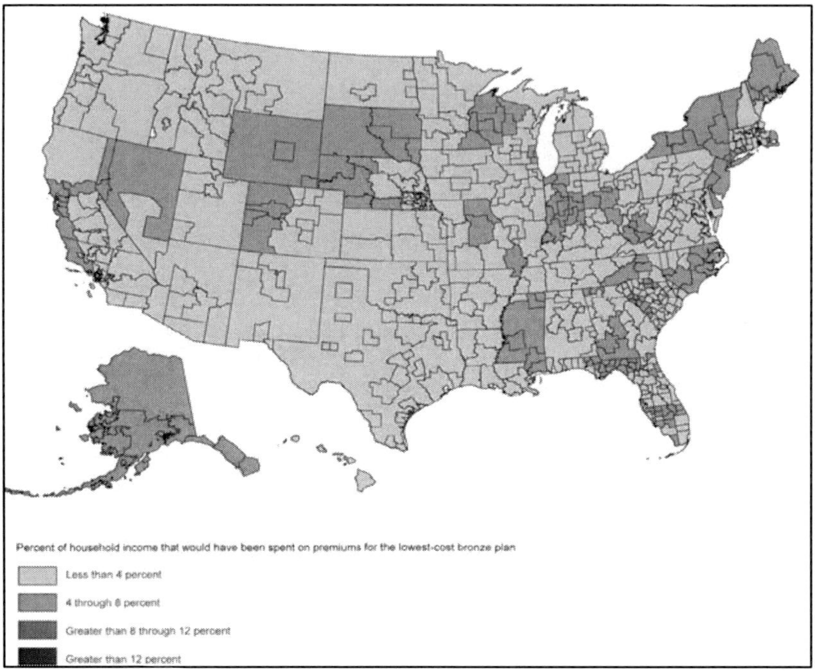

Source: GAO analysis of The Henry J. Kaiser Family Foundation data and New York state individual exchange data (data); Map Resources (map). | GAO 15-312

Note: Depending on the portion of health care costs expected to be paid by the health plan, qualified health plans are categorized into one of the following "metal tiers": bronze, silver, gold or platinum. Bronze plans cover an average of 60 percent of health care costs, silver plans cover 70 percent, gold plans cover 80 percent, and platinum plans cover 90 percent. The boundary lines depict the rating areas within each state except for Alaska. In Alaska, the boundary lines depict the three-digit zip codes in the state. In addition, due to how two zip codes are defined in Idaho, there are two areas in the state that were not assigned to a rating area and thus were left blank.

Figure 7. Percentage of Household Income That Would Have to Be Spent on Premiums for the Lowest-Cost Bronze Plan for a 27-Year-Old Individual with Household Income at 500 Percent of the Federal Poverty Level (2014).

Source: GAO analysis of The Henry J. Kaiser Family Foundation data and New York state individual exchange data (data); Map Resources (map). | GAO 15-312

Note: Depending on the portion of health care costs expected to be paid by the health plan, qualified health plans are categorized into one of the following "metal tiers": bronze, silver, gold or platinum. Bronze plans cover an average of 60 percent of health care costs, silver plans cover 70 percent, gold plans cover 80 percent, and platinum plans cover 90 percent. The boundary lines depict the rating areas within each state except for Alaska. In Alaska, the boundary lines depict the three-digit zip codes in the state. In addition, due to how two zip codes are defined in Idaho, there are two areas in the state that were not assigned to a rating area and thus were left blank.

Figure 8. Percentage of Household Income That Would Have to Be Spent on Premiums for the Lowest-Cost Bronze Plan for a 27-Year-Old Individual with Household Income at 600 Percent of the Federal Poverty Level (2014).

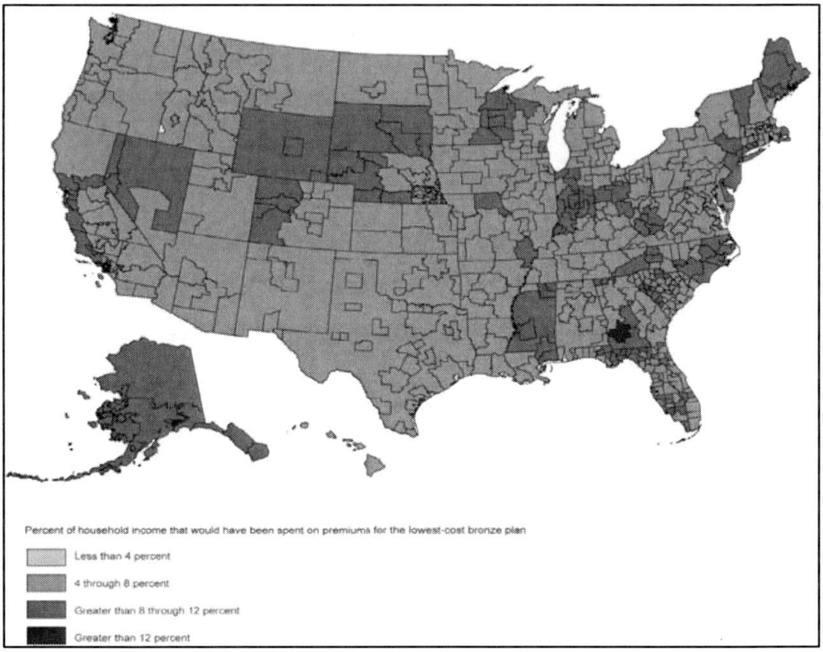

Source: GAO analysis of The Henry J. Kaiser Family Foundation data and New York state individual exchange data (data); Map Resources (map). | GAO 15-312

Note: Depending on the portion of health care costs expected to be paid by the health plan, qualified health plans are categorized into one of the following "metal tiers": bronze, silver, gold or platinum. Bronze plans cover an average of 60 percent of health care costs, silver plans cover 70 percent, gold plans cover 80 percent, and platinum plans cover 90 percent. The boundary lines depict the rating areas within each state except for Alaska. In Alaska, the boundary lines depict the three-digit zip codes in the state. In addition, due to how two zip codes are defined in Idaho, there are two areas in the state that were not assigned to a rating area and thus were left blank.

Figure 9. Percentage of Household Income That Would Have to Be Spent on Premiums for the Lowest-Cost Bronze Plan for a 40-Year-Old Married Couple with Two Children Under 21-Years-Old and Have Household Income at 450 Percent of the Federal Poverty Level (2014).

Source: GAO analysis of The Henry J. Kaiser Family Foundation data and New York state individual exchange data (data); Map Resources (map). | GAO 15-312

Note: Depending on the portion of health care costs expected to be paid by the health plan, qualified health plans are categorized into one of the following "metal tiers": bronze, silver, gold or platinum. Bronze plans cover an average of 60 percent of health care costs, silver plans cover 70 percent, gold plans cover 80 percent, and platinum plans cover 90 percent. The boundary lines depict the rating areas within each state except for Alaska. In Alaska, the boundary lines depict the three-digit zip codes in the state. In addition, due to how two zip codes are defined in Idaho, there are two areas in the state that were not assigned to a rating area and thus were left blank.

Figure 10. Percentage of Household Income That Would Have to Be Spent on Premiums for the Lowest-Cost Bronze Plan for a 40-Year-Old Married Couple with Two Children Under 21-Years-Old and Have Household Income at 500 Percent of the Federal Poverty Level (2014).

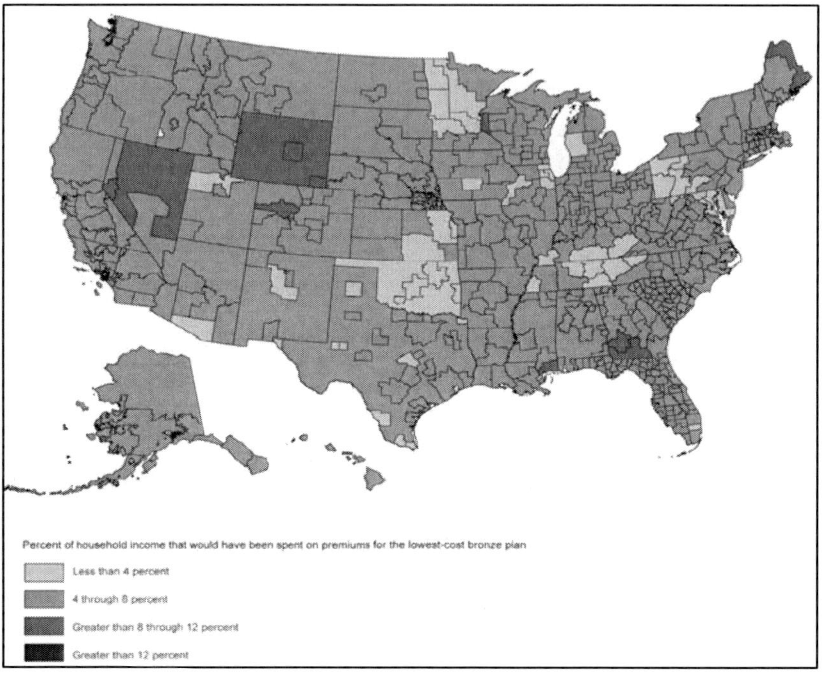

Source: GAO analysis of The Henry J. Kaiser Family Foundation data and New York state individual exchange data (data); Map Resources (map). | GAO 15-312

Note: Depending on the portion of health care costs expected to be paid by the health plan, qualified health plans are categorized into one of the following "metal tiers": bronze, silver, gold or platinum. Bronze plans cover an average of 60 percent of health care costs, silver plans cover 70 percent, gold plans cover 80 percent, and platinum plans cover 90 percent. The boundary lines depict the rating areas within each state except for Alaska. In Alaska, the boundary lines depict the three-digit zip codes in the state. In addition, due to how two zip codes are defined in Idaho, there are two areas in the state that were not assigned to a rating area and thus were left blank.

Figure 11. Percentage of Household Income That Would Have to Be Spent on Premiums for the Lowest-Cost Bronze Plan for a 40-Year-Old Married Couple with Two Children Under 21-Years-Old and Have Household Income at 600 Percent of the Federal Poverty Level (2014).

End Notes

[1] M. E. Martinez and R. A. Cohen, *Health Insurance Coverage: Early Release of Estimates from the National Health Interview Survey, January–June 2014* (Hyattsville, Md.: National Center for Health Statistics, 2014); and *Health Insurance Coverage: Early Release of Estimates from the National Health Interview Survey, January – March 2009,* (Hyattsville, Md.: National Center for Health Statistics, 2009).

The "nonelderly" refers to adults under age 65. In this report, we refer to nonelderly adults when we discuss those who are uninsured.

[2] The Henry J. Kaiser Family Foundation, *Distribution of the Nonelderly Uninsured by Federal Poverty Level*, accessed Jan. 5, 2015, http://kff.org/uninsured/state- indicator/distribution-by-fpl-2.

The FPL is an amount updated annually by the Department of Health and Human Services (HHS) to set eligibility for various means-tested programs.

[3] Pub. L. No. 111-148, §§ 1501, 10106, 124 Stat. 119, 242, 907 (2010), as amended by the Health Care and Education Reconciliation Act of 2010 (HCERA), Pub. L. No. 111-152, §§ 1002, 1004, 124 Stat. 1029, 1032, 1034 (2010) (codified at 26 U.S.C. § 5000A). In this report, references to PPACA include any amendments made by HCERA.

[4] Health insurance coverage that provides limited benefits, such as dental-only coverage, or Medicaid coverage that provides less than full benefits, such as Medicaid plans that cover only family planning, does not constitute minimum essential coverage.

Medicare is a federal health insurance program for individuals aged 65 and older, individuals under age 65 with certain disabilities, and individuals diagnosed with end-stage renal disease. Medicare Part A covers inpatient medical benefits. Other Medicare programs cover different goods and services.

[5] PPACA required the establishment of exchanges in each state by Jan. 1, 2014. In states that did not elect to operate their own state-based exchange, PPACA required the federal government to establish and operate an exchange in the state, known as federally facilitated exchanges. Pub. L. No. 111-148, §§ 1311(b), 1321(c), 124 Stat. 119 at 173, 186.

Our report assumed that individuals in all states could potentially be eligible for the premium tax credit, regardless of whether they purchased insurance through a state- based exchange or a federally facilitated exchange, consistent with the final rule issued by the Internal Revenue Service. *See* Health Insurance Premium Tax Credit, preamble 1.f and regulations to be codified at 26 C.F.R. §§ 1.36B-0 et seq.; 77 Fed. Reg. 30377, 30378, 30385 (May 23, 2012). The U.S. Supreme Court will consider whether PPACA authorizes the premium tax credit for individuals who purchase coverage through federally facilitated exchanges. *See* King v. Burwell, 759 F.3d 358 (4th Cir. 2014), *cert. granted*, 135 S. Ct. 475 (Nov. 7, 2014) (No. 14-114).

[6] Individuals who receive APTC must file federal income tax returns to reconcile the amount of the premium tax credit allowed based on reported income with the amount of the premium tax credit received in advance (APTC). An individual whose premium tax credit for the taxable year exceeds the individual's APTC payments may receive the excess as an income tax refund. An individual whose APTC payments for the taxable year exceed the individual's premium tax credit owes the excess as an additional income tax liability, subject to certain caps. 26 C.F.R. § 1.36B-4.

[7] Pub. L. No. 111-148, §§ 1421, 10105, 124 Stat. 119 at 237, 906 (codified at 26 U.S.C. § 45R).

[8] PPACA adjusts the thresholds at which premiums become unaffordable to reflect the excess of the rate of premium growth over the rate of income growth for the preceding calendar year. In 2015, the threshold at which premiums are unaffordable for purposes of determining an exemption from the requirement to have minimum essential coverage rose from 8 percent of household income to 8.05 percent. Similarly, the threshold at which an employee's share of

ESI premiums are considered unaffordable for purposes of APTC eligibility rose from 9.5 percent to 9.56 percent.

[9] PPACA also mandated that GAO review what is known about the effects of lowering the employer-sponsored insurance (ESI) affordability threshold. We discuss this topic in appendix I.

[10] This report discusses the advance premium tax credit rather than the premium tax credit because complete information on the premium tax credit was not available during the period of our review. In particular, individuals who received the APTC must, when filing their 2014 federal income tax returns, reconcile the amount of the premium tax credit allowed based on their reported income with the amount of the premium tax credit received in advance based on their anticipated income at the time of enrollment. Because our work preceded the reconciliation process, the only data available for our analysis was APTC data, not the reconciled amounts.

[11] GAO, *Small Employer Health Tax Credit: Factors Contributing to Low Use and Complexity*, GAO-12-549 (Washington, D.C.: May 14, 2012).

[12] Similarly, families are exempt when the lowest-cost health plan available to the family exceeds 8 percent of household income. For purposes of the individual mandate, household income is the taxpayer's modified adjusted gross income, plus that of every other individual in a family for whom an individual can properly claim a personal exemption deduction and who is required to file a federal income tax return. Modified adjusted gross income is a tax-based definition of income established in PPACA. See 26 U.S.C. § 5000A(c)(4)(B). Other exemptions may be available for certain eligible individuals, such as those determined to have suffered certain hardships, members of Native American tribes, and those who qualify for an exemption for religious reasons.

[13] PPACA requires the insurance plans offered under an exchange, known as qualified health plans, to provide a package of essential health benefits—including coverage for specific service categories, such as ambulatory care, prescription drugs, and hospitalization. In addition to these categories, states may require or restrict coverage of other benefits by qualified health plans. Pub. L. No. 111-148, §§ 1311(d), 10104(e)(1), 124 Stat. 119 at 176, 900.

[14] Some states that elected not to establish a state-based exchange entered into a partnership with the Department of Health and Human Services' (HHS) Centers for Medicare & Medicaid Services in which HHS establishes and operates the exchange while states assist HHS in carrying out certain functions of the exchange. Because a partnership exchange is a variation of a federally facilitated exchange, we include partnership states as federally facilitated exchange states in this report. In addition, in 2014, two states— Idaho and New Mexico—operated their own exchange, but enrollees signed up for health insurance through the federal website, http://www.healthcare.gov. The term "state" in this report includes the District of Columbia.

[15] 42 U.S.C. § 18022(d). In addition to these metal tiers, catastrophic plans are available to those under 30 years of age or to those who are exempt from the requirement to have minimum essential coverage because of a hardship or because the lowest-cost plan available would cost more than 8 percent of one's household income. Catastrophic plans' actuarial value must be lower than that of a bronze plan, so these plans have the highest level of cost sharing, although they cover preventive care at no cost. Enrollees are not eligible for the APTC.

[16] These cost-sharing provisions apply only to the essential health benefits and other goods and services that insurers cover. Goods and services that are not covered may cause additional expenses to be incurred.

[17] In 2013 in most states, applicable laws allowed broader variation for age and also allowed variation for other factors, such as health status and gender, which PPACA prohibited in 2014. See GAO, *Private Health Insurance: The Range of Base Premiums in the Individual Market by County in January 2013* (Washington D.C., Sept. 5, 2014) GAO-14-772R.

[18] Household income is the taxpayer's modified adjusted gross income, plus that of every other individual in a family for whom an individual can properly claim a personal exemption deduction and who is required to file a federal income tax return. For purposes of the premium tax credit, and in contrast to the individual mandate, modified adjusted gross income includes nontaxable Social Security benefits. See 26 U.S.C. § 36B(d)(2)(B); 26 U.S.C. § 5000A(c)(4)(C).

Certain lawfully present immigrants with incomes below 100 percent of FPL who would eligible for Medicaid but for their immigration status are eligible for the APTC.

[19] The second-lowest-cost silver plan available is the plan that applies to a taxpayer's "coverage family." Members of the coverage family are those for whom a taxpayer claims a personal exemption and who are enrolled in a qualified health plan through an exchange and not eligible for other minimum essential coverage.

[20] If the amount of the credit is larger than the premium itself, the enrollee pays no premium. Conversely, if the premium cost is less than the percentage of household income an individual is required to contribute based on FPL, then the individual will not receive a tax credit.

[21] 42 U.S.C. § 18071.

[22] American Indians and Alaska Natives are eligible for cost-sharing assistance up to 300 percent of the FPL.

[23] Specifically, PPACA authorizes states to expand eligibility for Medicaid to most non- elderly adults whose income is at or below 133 percent of the FPL. PPACA also specifies that an income disregard in the amount of 5 percent of the FPL be deducted from an individual's income when determining Medicaid eligibility, which effectively raises the income eligibility threshold for newly eligible Medicaid recipients in expansion states to 138 percent of the FPL.

[24] See 26 U.S.C. § 36B(c)(1)(A). The minimum income levels applicable to APTC also apply to federal cost-sharing subsidies, which reduce out-of-pocket costs for such things as copayments for physician visits or prescription drugs. See 42 U.S.C. § 18071(b)(2).

[25] 26 U.S.C. § 4980H. These requirements are being phased in over time. In 2015, employers with between 50 to 99 full-time equivalent employees are exempt from the requirement. Employers with more than 100 full-time equivalent employees must offer qualifying health insurance coverage to 70 percent of full-time employees in 2015. In 2016, employers with 50 or more full-time equivalent employees will be required to offer qualifying coverage to 95 percent of their full-time employees. Employers out of compliance will be subject to an annual tax penalty of $2,000 times the number of full-time employees minus 30, if one of their full-time employees receives the APTC to purchase health insurance through the individual exchanges. See *Shared Responsibility for Employers Regarding Health Coverage*, 79 Fed. Reg. 8544 (Feb. 12, 2014).

[26] 26 U.S.C. § 45R.

[27] In 2014, 18 states chose to operate state-based SHOPs while 33 states opted for a federally facilitated SHOP.

[28] B. D. Sommers, T. Musco, K. Finegold, M. Z., Gunja, et al. "Health Reform and Changes in Health Insurance Coverage in 2014," *The New England Journal of Medicine*, vol. 371, no. 9 (Aug. 28, 2014).

[29] Other factors or provisions in the PPACA could have also affected changes in the rate of uninsured, including the requirement to maintain minimum essential coverage or pay a tax penalty (i.e., the individual mandate), the requirement that some large employers offer health insurance to full-time employees, or individual market reforms that prohibited issuers from denying individuals coverage and setting rates based on individuals' health status.

[30] Department of Health and Human Services (HHS), Office of the Assistant Secretary for Planning and Evaluation, *Health Insurance Marketplace: Summary Enrollment Report for the Initial Open Enrollment Period* (Washington, D.C.: May 1, 2014). As of November 2014, HHS reported that 6.7 million individuals had enrolled in a health plan through the

individual exchanges, after accounting for effectuated enrollment—that is, individuals who had selected a plan and paid their premiums—and excluding enrollment in dental plans. Of these individuals, 85 percent were deemed eligible for the APTC. As of January 2015, however, HHS had not revised its summary statistics on the amount of APTC that eligible individuals had received or the amount that the APTC reduced premiums for those eligible.

[31] Department of Health and Human Services, *Health Insurance Marketplace*; and Department of Health and Human Services, Office of the Assistant Secretary for Planning and Evaluation, *Premium Affordability, Competition, and Choice in Health Insurance Marketplace, 2014* (Washington, D.C.: June 18, 2014). In its analysis of the amount of APTC that individuals received and the extent to which it reduced premiums, HHS included data from the 34 federally facilitated exchanges as well as 2 state-based exchanges—Idaho and New Mexico—that used the federal website, http://www.healthcare.gov, for exchange enrollment in 2014.

[32] Department of Health and Human Services, *Premium Affordability*. Of those who were deemed eligible for an APTC when they selected a health plan through 1 of the 34 federally facilitated exchanges or 1 of the 2 state-based exchanges that used the federal website, http://www.healthcare.gov, for enrollment in 2014, most (76 percent) selected a silver plan, followed by 15 percent who selected a bronze plan, 6 percent who selected a gold plan, and 3 percent who selected a platinum plan. Department of Health and Human Services, *Health Insurance Marketplace*. Individuals with household incomes between 100 and 250 percent of the FPL—those eligible to receive both the APTC and the cost-sharing reduction subsidies—may have been encouraged to select silver because, by selecting a bronze plan, they would have become ineligible to receive the cost-sharing reduction subsidies.

[33] Thirteen percent of individuals who selected a health plan through 1 of the 34 federally facilitated exchanges or 1 of the 2 state-based exchanges that used the federal website, http://www.healthcare.gov, for enrollment in 2014 and were deemed eligible for the APTC had their monthly premiums reduced to between $101 and $150 ($1,212 to $1,800 annually), and 18 percent had an after-APTC monthly premium amount greater than $150 (greater than $1,800 annually). Department of Health and Human Services, *Premium Affordability*.

[34] The survey examined changes in the rate of nonelderly uninsured adults by income and found that, between 2013 and 2014, the uninsured rate declined by 2 percentage points among those with household incomes between 250 and 399 percent of the FPL— individuals eligible for a smaller APTC amount and ineligible for cost-sharing reduction subsidies. By comparison, the uninsured rate declined by 10 percentage points among those with household incomes between 138 and 249 percent of the FPL—individuals eligible for a larger APTC amount as well as cost-sharing reduction subsidies. S. R. Collins, P. W. Rasmussen, and M. M. Doty, *Gaining Ground: Americans' Health Insurance Coverage after the Affordable Care Act's First Open Enrollment Period* (New York: The Commonwealth Fund, 2014).

[35] Department of Health and Human Services, Office of the Assistant Secretary for Planning and Evaluation, *Health Plan Choice and Premiums in the 2015 Health Insurance Marketplace* (Washington, D.C.: Dec. 4, 2014).

[36] For example, one study that measured the change in premiums between 2014 and 2015 found that, while premiums for the lowest-cost bronze plan increased by an average of 4 percent, they increased by up to 43 percent in western counties of Minnesota and declined by at most 40 percent in Summit County, Colorado. C. Cox, L. Levitt, G. Claxton, R. Ma, and R. Duddy-Tenbrunsel, *Analysis of 2015 Premium Changes in the Affordable Care Act's Health Insurance Marketplaces* (Menlo Park, Calif.: Jan. 6, 2015).

[37] Also, as premiums are influenced by underlying costs of health care, there remains uncertainty as to whether lower than historical trends in health care cost growth in recent years will continue in future years.

[38] For 78 percent of individuals who selected a silver plan in 2014, the lowest-cost silver plan in 2015 cost less than their 2014 plan. Similarly, for 78 percent of who selected a bronze plan in 2014, the lowest-cost bronze plan in 2015 was cheaper than their 2014 plan. Department of Health and Human Services, *Health Plan Choice.*

[39] L. Hamel, B. DiJulio, J. Firth, M. Brodie, *Kaiser Health Tracking Poll: November 2014* (Menlo Park, Calif.: The Henry J. Kaiser Family Foundation, 2014); A. Bhardwaj, E. Coe, J. Cordina, and R. Saha, *Individual Market: Insights Into Consumer Behavior at the End of Open Enrollment* (New York: McKinsey Center for U.S. Health System Reform, 2014); and A. Schatzer, G. M. Kenney, S. K. Long, K. Hemstead, et al. *Who Are the Remaining Uninsured As of June 2014?* (Washington, D.C.: The Urban Institute, 2014). In addition, publicly available summary results from the fourth survey showed that of all nonelderly adults surveyed who reported that they shopped on an exchange for a health insurance plan, 54 percent said that it was "very difficult or impossible" or "somewhat difficult" to find a plan they could afford. P. W. Rasmussen, S. R. Collins, M. M. Doty, and S. Beutel, *Are Americans Finding Affordable Coverage in the Health Insurance Marketplaces? Results from the Commonwealth Fund Affordable Care Act Survey* (New York: The Commonwealth Fund, September 2014).

[40] Collins et al., *Gaining Ground*; L. Hamel, J. Firth, B. DiJulio, and K. Brodie, *Kaiser Health Tracking Poll: October 2014* (Menlo Park, Calif.: The Henry J. Kaiser Family Foundation, 2014); and Schatzer et al., *Who Are the Remaining Uninsured.* In addition, publicly available summary results from the fourth survey found that 44 percent of the uninsured surveyed who were likely eligible for financial assistance were aware of the APTC. Bhardwaj et al., *Individual Market.*

[41] See appendix II for additional information about the response rates, sample sizes, and margins of error of early surveys cited in this report.

[42] The first large data set that covers the full first year of enrollment in the exchanges will become available in June 2015 with the release of complete 2014 National Health Interview Survey data, though precise income data in this survey will not become available until August 2015.

[43] As of September 15, 2014, HHS officials reported that at least 363,000 individuals who selected a health plan through the exchanges had not yet submitted required documentation. Department of Health and Human Services, Centers for Medicare and Medicaid Services (CMS), *CMS Update on Consumers Who Have Data Matching Issues,* Press Release (Washington, D.C.: Sept. 15, 2014). Individuals may enroll in coverage through an exchange during a special enrollment period outside of open enrollment due to a qualifying life event, such as a change in family status (e.g., marriage or birth of a child) or the loss of other health coverage, such as ESI.

[44] HHS included data from 2 of the 17 state-based exchanges—Idaho and New Mexico— in its summary data on the amount of APTC received by individuals who selected a health plan and were deemed eligible for the APTC. These two state-based exchanges used the federal website, http://www.healthcare.gov, for their 2014 exchange enrollment.

[45] Individuals who receive APTC must file federal income tax returns in order to reconcile the amount of the premium tax credit allowed based on reported income with the amount of the premium tax credit received in advance (APTC). An individual whose premium tax credit for the taxable year exceeds the individual's APTC payments may receive the excess as an income tax refund. An individual whose APTC payments for the taxable year exceed the individual's premium tax credit owes the excess as an additional income tax liability, subject to certain caps. 26 C.F.R. § 1.36B-4.

[46] Complete data on the number of entities that claimed a tax credit are generally not available until sometime after the tax year in question because of the complex nature of filing and reconciling taxes.

[47] Data limitations made these estimates necessarily rough. See GAO9.

[48] The total amount of credit claimed by employers continued to be lower than experts had projected. In March 2012, the Congressional Budget Office (CBO) and the Joint Committee on Taxation estimated that the cost of the credit would be $1 billion in 2012. This estimate was previously $5 billion in 2012. In 2012, employers claimed about $507 million in credits compared to $645 million in 2011 and $468 million in 2010.

[49] See GAO 12. In addition, we found no peer reviewed studies that examined whether or not the small employer tax credit affected employers' decisions to offer health insurance or lowered the costs of ESI in the last four years.

[50] The average annual wages were $25,000 or less through 2013. The maximum average wage limit is indexed for inflation beginning in 2014.

[51] Through 2013, small for-profit employers could receive up to 35 percent (nonprofit entities up to 25 percent) of their base payments for employee health insurance premiums. These portions rose to 50 percent and 35 percent, respectively, starting in 2014.

[52] The Medical Expenditure Panel Survey (MEPS) estimated that in 2013, 86 percent of employers who may otherwise be eligible for the full credit did not offer health insurance. This MEPS statistic is based on employers—both for profit and nonprofit—with fewer than 10 employees that pay annual wages of $24,000 or less to over half of their employees. Further, 6 percent of employers that may be eligible for the partial credit did not offer insurance. This MEPS statistic is based on employers—both for profit and nonprofit—with 10 to 24 employees that pay annual wages of $24,000 or less to over half of their employees. Because the employers eligible for the partial credit can pay up to $50,000 in wages, this is a less precise estimate than using MEPS to estimate insurance offerings for the full credit.

[53] See also GAO12.

[54] See GAO12-13.

[55] The IRS has stated that in 2014, small employers in certain counties in Wisconsin and Washington where SHOP plans are not offered may be eligible for the tax credit if they offer coverage that would have qualified for the credit prior to January 1, 2014. See Internal Revenue Service, Section 45R – *Transition Relief with Respect to the Tax Credit for Employee Health Insurance Expenses of Certain Small Employers*, Internal Revenue Bulletin: 2014-2 (Washington, D.C.: Jan. 6, 2014). Similarly, the IRS has stated that in 2015, small employers in certain counties in Iowa where SHOP plans are not offered may be eligible for the tax credit if they offer coverage that would have qualified for the credit prior to January 1, 2014. See Internal Revenue Service, Section 45R-2015 – *Guidance with Respect to the Tax Credit from Employee Health Insurance Expenses of Certain Small Employers*, Internal Revenue Bulletin: 2015-6 (Washington, D.C.: Feb. 9, 2015).

[56] GAO, *Small Business Health Insurance Exchanges: Low Initial Enrollment Likely due to Multiple, Evolving Factors*, GAO-15-58 (Washington, D.C.: Nov. 13, 2014), 12.

[57] Until 2016, states have the option to define small employers either as employers with 100 or fewer full-time equivalent employees or employers with 50 or fewer full-time equivalent employees. In contrast, to qualify for the small employer tax credit, employers must employ fewer than 25 full-time equivalent employees in the tax year (excluding certain employees, such as business owners and their family members).

[58] GAO15.

[59] In a previous report, we found that the reasons for the low enrollment included the delay of some expected SHOP features. For example, online enrollment was not available for states with federally facilitated SHOP exchanges, and few SHOP exchanges offered employees a choice of plans. In addition, we reported that the small employer tax credit provided an insufficient incentive for employers to sign up. GAO20.

[60] K.G. Carman and C. Eibner, *Changes in Health Insurance Enrollment Since 2013: Evidence from the RAND Health Reform Opinion Study* (Santa Monica, Calif.: RAND Corporation, 2014).

ESI generally qualifies as minimum essential coverage. However, according to experts we interviewed, some employers may offer plans with few benefits that do not meet the requirement that ESI cover 60 percent of the actuarial value of health care for the average person. Such plans generally cover only preventive services, according to these experts. Employees and their families who enroll in such plans are not subject to the penalty for failing to maintain minimum essential coverage. However, ESI plans that do not cover the minimum 60-percent actuarial value of health care costs are not affordable for purposes of determining eligibility for the APTC, and employers offering only these plans may be subject to a penalty if an employee obtains health insurance through an exchange and receives the APTC.

[61] CBO estimated that up to 500,000 of an estimated 156 million individuals were offered unaffordable ESI in 2014 and enrolled in plans through the exchanges, suggesting that most with access to ESI are offered affordable coverage. Congressional Budget Office, *Updated Estimates of the Effects of the Insurance Coverage Provisions of the Affordable Care Act* (Washington, D.C., April 2014). Other researchers have reported similar estimates. See appendix I for more information.

[62] With financial assistance from the APTC, the cost of health insurance premiums for those eligible is reduced to an amount considered affordable—that is, the cost of premiums for the second lowest-cost silver plan are capped at between 2 and 9.5 percent of household income, depending on one's income.

[63] Carman and Eibner, *Changes in Health Insurance*; and Department of Health and Human Services, *Health Insurance Marketplace.* Minimum essential coverage generally includes Medicaid. However, some Medicaid enrollees may have had coverage under limited benefit plans that do not qualify as minimum essential coverage, such as Medicaid plans that cover only family planning. In addition, minimum essential coverage generally includes health plans offered through the exchanges with the exception of catastrophic plans.

[64] Carman and Eibner, Changes in Health Insurance. TRICARE plans require no premiums or up to $548 annually for a family plan, depending on the individuals' military status, type of TRICARE plan, and where they choose to receive their care. Four percent of nonelderly adults—which is included in the 14 percent of nonelderly adults who were insured through other sources—obtained their coverage through the individual market outside the exchanges. Information about the affordability of such plans is not available.

[65] Carman and Eibner, *Changes in Health Insurance*. Results from early surveys have estimated that between 12.4 and 17.0 percent of nonelderly adults were uninsured as of early 2014, though all surveys consistently show that the rate of uninsured has declined since 2013, ranging from a decline of 3.4 to 5.3 percentage points. See Long et al., *Taking Stock*; Collins, et al., *Gaining Ground*; Sommers et al., *Health Reform and Changes*; and Martinez and Cohen, *Health Insurance Coverage.*

[66] Individuals qualify for the affordability exemption if the required amount that they would have to contribute for the lowest-cost, self-only plan available to them costs more than 8 percent of their household income. Individuals could also be exempt from the requirement to maintain minimum essential coverage because they were members of Native American tribes, individuals with qualifying religious exemptions, or received a hardship exemption. In addition to those exempt, CBO also estimated that some people who lack minimum essential coverage will try to avoid penalties when filing their income tax returns. Congressional Budget Office, *Payments of Penalties for Being Uninsured Under the Affordable Care Act: 2014 Update* (Washington, D.C.: June 2014).

[67] Some of the uninsured may have access to affordable coverage but chose not to take- up that coverage. For example, one study estimated that 3 percent of the uninsured (8.1 million) were eligible for Medicaid and 4 percent (10.9 million) were eligible for the APTC. Another 2 percent (7.3 million), though they had access to affordable coverage, would have to pay a penalty for failing to maintain minimum essential coverage. L. J. Blumberg, M. Buettgens, J. Feder, *The Individual Mandate in Perspective: Timely Analysis of Immediate Health*

Policy Issues (Washington, D.C.: The Urban Institute, 2012). In addition, some people who were insured in 2014 may have had coverage that did not qualify as minimum essential coverage, such as Medicaid partial-benefit coverage.

[68] Some states permit certain nonelderly adults with incomes greater than 100 percent of the FPL to enroll in Medicaid, such as those who are pregnant or disabled.

[69] Individuals are eligible to purchase a catastrophic plan if they are under age 30 or the lowest-cost bronze plan available costs more than 8 percent of their household income. In Medicaid nonexpansion states where a catastrophic plan was available, a 27-year-old individual with household income at 99 percent of the FPL would have had to spend between 8.4 and 27.5 percent of household income on the cheapest catastrophic plan. A 27-year-old individual with lower household income would have had to spend an even larger percentage of their household income on such a plan. In addition, insurers are permitted to charge higher premiums based on age and family size, so older individuals or individuals with a larger family would have had to spend an even larger percentage of their household income on either the lowest-cost catastrophic or bronze plan.

[70] R. Garfield, A. Damico, J. Stephens, and S. Rouhani, *The Coverage Gap: Uninsured Poor Adults in States that Do Not Expand Medicaid—An Update* (Menlo Park, Calif.: The Henry J. Kaiser Family Foundation, 2014).

[71] Medicaid and CHIP Payment and Access Commission, *Report to the Congress on Medicaid and CHIP* (Washington, D.C.: March 2014). AHRQ's estimate was conducted at the request of the Medicaid and CHIP Payment and Access Commission and published in its report.

[72] In addition, for some individuals, even with financial assistance from the APTC, premiums for the lowest-cost bronze plan available in the individual exchanges may have exceeded 8 percent of household income in 2014, depending on the difference in the cost of premiums from the reference plan. However, this may have only occurred in some rating areas. For example, in just 8 out of the 501 rating areas (2 percent), a 60-year-old individual with household income at 400 percent of FPL would have had to pay greater than 8 percent of their household income on the lowest-cost bronze plan after accounting for the APTC. And, in 52 of 501 rating areas (10 percent), a family of four with two parents aged 40 years old and two children under 21 years of age with household income at 400 percent of the FPL would have had to spend greater than 8 percent of its household income on the lowest-cost bronze plan after accounting for the APTC.

[73] Shartzer et al., *Who Are the Remaining Uninsured*. Some individuals without affordable ESI who have household incomes greater than 400 percent of the FPL may have been able to afford health insurance coverage but chose instead to pay the penalty.

[74] Among individuals who selected a health plan without financial assistance from the APTC through 1 of the 34 federally facilitated exchanges or the 2 state-based exchanges that used the federal website, http://www.healthcare.gov, for enrollment in 2014, they were most likely to select a bronze plan than any other metal tier. For example, 33 percent of those who selected a health plan without financial assistance from the APTC through these 36 exchanges selected a bronze plan while 25 percent selected a silver plan and 12 percent selected a catastrophic plan. Of those who selected a catastrophic plan through these 36 exchanges, most (85 percent) were under age 35. Department of Health and Human Services, *Health Insurance Marketplace*.

[75] Under PPACA, issuers are prohibited from setting premium rates based on an individual's health status. However, issuers are permitted to set rates based on one's age, though rates based on age cannot vary by more than a 3:1 ratio under PPACA. States may have additional restrictions. For example, New York and Vermont have a 1:1 age rating ratio.

[76] Under PPACA, the rating area is the lowest geographic level by which health insurance premiums are permitted to vary. However, according to one expert we interviewed, plans may not be offered in all service areas throughout a rating area. For example, a health insurer could offer a health plan in all but one or two counties within a rating area. As a result, the lowest-cost plan available could vary within a rating area.

[77] Early survey data has shown the largest declines in the rate of uninsured between 2013 and early 2014 occurred among younger adults. See Martinez and Cohen, *Health Insurance Coverage*; Collins et al., *Gaining Ground*; Sommers et al., *Health Reform and Changes*; and Long et al., *Taking Stock*. However, most of the uninsured in 2014 were age 18 to 34 (42 percent) followed by individuals aged 35 to 44 (19 percent) and individuals age 45 to 64 (12 percent). Martinez and Cohen, *Health Insurance Coverage*.

[78] In contrast, in the least expensive rating area for a 60-year-old individual (counties near Rochester, NY), the annual premium for the lowest-cost bronze plan was $2,575, which would have been considered affordable for a 60-year-old individual at any income level over 400 percent of the FPL.

[79] In contrast, in counties near Minneapolis and St. Paul, MN, the least expensive rating area for such an individual, the annual premiums for the lowest-cost bronze plan were $1,132, which would have been affordable for such a family any income level.

[80] In contrast, in Comanche County, OK, the least expensive rating area for such a family, the annual premiums for the lowest-cost bronze plan were $4,397, which would have been affordable for such a family at any income level greater than 400 percent of the FPL.

[81] Enrollees who experience changes can file with an exchange to report that their income has changed. Alternatively, when enrollees file taxes, the APTC amount will be reconciled with their actual income for the preceding year.

GAO is currently examining issues related to individuals' movement between the exchanges and Medicaid.

[82] For example, one study examined changes in household income. It found that 2 percent of adults in households with incomes between 133 and 199 percent of the FPL in 2005 had incomes over 400 percent in the following year, and 15 percent of adults with incomes between 200 and 399 percent of the FPL had incomes over 400 percent in the following year. If the same income changes occurred in 2014, those households would be ineligible for the APTC. See P. Farley Short, K. Swartz, N. Uberoi, and D. Graefe, *Realizing Health Reform's Potential: Maintaining Coverage, Affordability, and Shared Responsibility When Income and Employment Change* (Washington, D.C.: The Commonwealth Fund, May 2011). Some of these households may enroll in ESI, even if they are income-eligible for the APTC or Medicaid.

[83] S. R. Collins, R. Robertson, T. Garber, and M. M. Doty, *Gaps in Health Insurance: Why So Many Americans Experience Breaks in Coverage and How the Affordable Care Act Will Help* (Washington, D.C.: The Commonwealth Fund, April 2012).

[84] This limit does not include premiums, balance billing amounts for non-network providers and other out-of-network cost-sharing, or spending for non-essential health benefits that are not covered by the plan.

[85] Exchange enrollees with incomes between 100 and 250 percent of the FPL are eligible for cost-sharing subsidies that reduce their maximum out-of-pocket costs if they are enrolled in a silver plan. Because silver plan premiums are higher than bronze plan premiums, some enrollees with low out-of-pocket costs may pay less overall by enrolling in a bronze plan without cost-sharing subsidies. Others with higher out-of-pocket costs would likely pay less overall in a silver plan with cost-sharing subsidies.

Insurers can choose one of two ways to reduce out-of-pocket spending for cost-sharing subsidy-eligible enrollees. Insurers can either reduce the total out-of-pocket spending limit to specified amounts, or insurers can design plans to meet higher actuarial values.

[86] Pub. L. No. 111-148, § 1401(c), 124 Stat. 119, 220 (2010).

[87] See appendix II for details on our search for studies.

[88] Employers out of compliance will be subject to an annual fine of $2,000 times the number of full-time employees minus 30. For example, in 2016, an employer with 50 full-time equivalents that did not offer insurance would be penalized $40,000.

[89] In contrast, another study separately estimated that about 10.5 million people are subject to the "family glitch"—that is, they are not eligible for the APTC or cost sharing subsidies

because one household member has an offer of self-only coverage that is affordable, as discussed earlier. Medicaid and CHIP Payment and Access Commission, *Report to the Congress on Medicaid and CHIP* (Washington, D.C.: March 2014). This study was conducted at the request of the Medicaid and CHIP Payment and Access Commission and published in its report.

[90] Agency for Healthcare Research Quality, *Employer and Worker Incentives in the Affordable Care Act: Insights from a Linked Employer-Employee Data Set* (Washington, D.C.: June 23, 2013). Using Medical Expenditure Panel Survey (MEPS) Household Component data, authors created synthetic workforces for each establishment in the MEPS Insurance Component. Estimates may be imprecise due to multiple sources of errors, including the error stemming from linking household and establishment data.

[91] Congressional Budget Office, *Updated Estimates of the Effects of the Insurance Coverage Provisions of the Affordable Care Act* (Washington, D.C.: Congressional Budget Office, April 2014).

[92] Researchers merged data from the MEPS Insurance Component, the March Current Population Survey as well as other data, and The Henry J. Kaiser Family Foundation premium data. This study has limitations as well, such as potential biases from various simplifying assumptions used for the analysis. For example, the researchers assumed that if an employee no longer received ESI, employers would fully pass on the savings from premiums to the employees. R. V. Burkhauser, S. Lyons, K. I. Simon, "The Importance of the Meaning and Measurement of 'Affordable' In the Affordable Care Act" (Cambridge, Mass.: National Bureau of Economic Research, Working Paper 17279, 2011).

[93] The Henry J. Kaiser Family Foundation and Health Research & Educational Trust, *Employer Health Benefits 2014 Annual Survey* (Washington, D.C.: The Henry J. Kaiser Family Foundation and Health Research & Educational Trust, 2014).

[94] For these and all studies cited in our report, we reviewed the methodologies of the studies to ensure they were sound and determined that they were sufficiently reliable for our purposes.

[95] Larger, more rigorous survey data that can be used to more accurately estimate individuals' health insurance status were not yet available at the time that we conducted our analyses.

[96] Experts we interviewed included representatives from: American Enterprise Institute; The Center for Health Insurance Reforms at Georgetown University; HHS's Agency for Healthcare Research and Quality, Center for Consumer Information and Insurance Oversight, Office of the Assistant Secretary of Planning and Evaluation, and the Office of the Actuary; the Congressional Budget Office; IRS; National Business Group on Health; National Federation of Independent Businesses; Pennsylvania State University; The Commonwealth Fund; The Henry J. Kaiser Family Foundation; The Urban Institute; and the University of Minnesota.

[97] Internal control is a process effected by an entity's oversight body, management, and other personnel that provides reasonable assurance that the objectives of an entity will be achieved.

[98] See GAO, *Small Employer Health Tax Credit: Factors Contributing to Low Use and Complexity*, GAO-12-549 (Washington, D.C.: May 14, 2012).

[99] PPACA required the establishment of exchanges in each state by January 1, 2014. In states that did not elect to operate their own state-based exchange, PPACA required the federal government to establish and operate an exchange in the state, known as federally facilitated exchanges. Some states that elected not to establish a state-based exchange entered into a partnership with the Department of Health and Human Services' (HHS) Centers for Medicare & Medicaid Services (CMS), in which HHS establishes and operates the exchange while states assist HHS in carrying out certain functions of the exchange. A partnership exchange is a variation of a federally facilitated exchange. In addition, in 2014, two states—Idaho and New Mexico—operated their own exchange but enrollees signed up for health insurance through the federal website, http://www.healthcare.gov, which populates CMS's Landscape file.

[100] We used the 2013 federal poverty level because 2014 eligibility for APTC and Medicaid was based on the 2013 level.

In: Health Insurance Affordability ...
Editor: Brittany Rodriquez

ISBN: 978-1-63482-931-1

Chapter 2

HEALTH INSURANCE PREMIUM CREDITS IN THE PATIENT PROTECTION AND AFFORDABLE CARE ACT (ACA) IN 2015*

Bernadette Fernandez

SUMMARY

New federal tax credits, authorized under the Patient Protection and Affordable Care Act (ACA; P.L. 111-148, as amended), first became available in 2014 to help certain individuals pay for health insurance. The tax credits apply toward premiums for private health plans offered through *exchanges* (also referred to as health insurance *marketplaces*). The ACA also established subsidies to reduce cost-sharing expenses.

Health insurance exchanges operate in every state and the District of Columbia (DC), per the ACA statute. Exchanges may be established and administered by states, the federal government, or a combination of both. Exchanges are not insurers, but they provide eligible individuals and small businesses with access to private health insurance plans. Generally, plans offered through the exchanges provide a comprehensive set of health services and meet all of the ACA's insurance market reforms, as applicable.

* This is an edited, reformatted and augmented version of a Congressional Research Service publication R43945, prepared for Members and Committees of Congress dated March 18, 2015.

The new premium credits established under the ACA are advanceable and refundable, meaning tax filers need not wait until the end of the tax year to benefit from the credit and may claim the full credit amount even if they have little or no federal income tax liability. Premium tax credits generally are available to individuals who enroll in an exchange plan; are part of a tax-filing unit; have household income between specified amounts; are not eligible for other forms of comprehensive health coverage; and are U.S. citizens or lawfully present residents. This report provides examples of hypothetical individuals and families that qualify for the premium credits. The examples use actual 2015 exchange premiums.

The amounts received in premium credits are based on federal income tax returns. These amounts are reconciled after individuals file their returns and can result in overpayment of premium credits if income increases, which must be repaid to the federal government. The ACA limits the amount of required repayments for lower-income enrollees.

In addition to premium credits, the ACA authorized new cost-sharing subsidies. Certain premium credit recipients also are eligible for reductions in their annual cost-sharing limits. Moreover, certain low-income individuals receive additional subsidies in the form of reduced cost-sharing requirements (e.g., lower deductibles).

New federal tax credits were authorized in the Patient Protection and Affordable Care Act (ACA; P.L. 111-148, as amended), to help certain individuals pay for health insurance coverage, beginning in 2014.[1] The tax credits apply toward premiums for private health plans offered through *exchanges* (also referred to as *health insurance marketplaces*). The ACA also authorized subsidies to reduce cost-sharing expenses.

This report describes the eligibility criteria applicable to the premium tax credits and cost-sharing subsidies, and the calculation method for the credit and subsidy amounts. It also highlights selected issues addressed in the final regulation and guidance on premium credits and indicates the status of implementation, where relevant data is available.

EXCHANGES AND PREMIUM CREDITS

Health insurance exchanges operate in every state and the District of Columbia (DC), per the ACA statute. Exchanges may be established and administered by states, the federal government (administered through the

Department of Health and Human Services [HHS]), or a combination of both.[2] Exchanges are not insurance companies; rather, they are *marketplaces* that offer private health plans to qualified individuals[3] and small businesses.[4] Generally, exchange plans provide a comprehensive set of health services and meet all of the ACA's insurance market reforms, as applicable.[5] In addition, most exchange plans comply with a requirement that measures how much a given plan will pay for a group of individuals (who vary in terms of medical use and expenses); that measure is referred to as actuarial value (AV).[6] Most exchange plans meet a specific AV, with each AV designated by a precious metal: bronze (actuarial value of 60%), silver (70%), gold (80%), and platinum (90%). For AVs, the higher the percentage, the lower the cost sharing, *on average*.[7]

Given that the ACA specifically requires exchanges to offer insurance options to individuals and small businesses, the ACA requires exchanges to be structured to assist these two different types of "customers." Consequently, there is an exchange to serve individuals and families, and another to serve small businesses (SHOP exchanges[8]) within each state. However, the ACA gives states the option to provide one exchange to serve both individuals and small businesses.[9]

Certain enrollees in the *individual* exchanges are eligible for premium assistance in the form of federal tax credits.[10] Such credits are not provided through the SHOP exchanges. The premium credit is an advanceable, refundable tax credit, meaning tax filers need not wait until the end of the tax year to benefit from the credit and may claim the full credit amount even if they have little or no federal income tax liability. Receiving the credits as advanced payments means that monthly insurance premiums will be automatically reduced by the credit amount. Therefore, the direct cost of insurance to an individual/family *generally* will be lower than the "advertised" cost for a given exchange plan.[11]

The Treasury Department (Treasury) promulgated final regulation on the premium credits on May 23, 2012.[12] The final regulation confirmed certain eligibility and other requirements, as specified in statute; such requirements are discussed in applicable sections of this report. In addition, the Internal Revenue Service (IRS) has issued guidance and other documentation (such as Q&As) relevant to premium credits.[13]

King vs. Burwell

On March 4, 2015, the Supreme Court heard oral arguments in King vs. Burwell.14 At issue in King and other similar legal challenges is whether the statutory language of the ACA allows the IRS to provide premium tax credits to residents of states that declined to establish health insurance exchanges. The issue is considered a significant one, not only because a majority of states have exchanges that were not established by the states, and millions of individuals residing in those states receive credits, but also because of the far-reaching implications of a potential loss of credits on the private market more broadly and implementation of other ACA provisions.

PREMIUM CREDIT ELIGIBILITY

The ACA specifies that premium credits will be available to "applicable taxpayers" in a "coverage month."[15]

An *applicable taxpayer* is an individual who

- is part of a tax-filing unit;
- is enrolled in a plan through an individual exchange; and
- has household income at or above 100% of the federal poverty level (FPL), but not more than 400% FPL.[16]

A *coverage month* refers to a month in which the applicable taxpayer paid for coverage offered through an exchange, not including any month in which the taxpayer was *eligible* for "minimum essential coverage" with exceptions.

These eligibility criteria are discussed in greater detail below.[17]

Part of a Tax-Filing Unit

Premium assistance is provided in the form of tax credits, which are administered through the tax system (although advance payments go directly to insurers).[18] The premium credit process requires qualifying individuals to file federal tax returns, even if their incomes are at levels that normally do not necessitate the filing of tax returns.

Married couples are required to file joint tax returns to claim the credit.[19] The final regulation includes special rules relating to the calculation and allocation of credit amounts due to changes in filing status during a given tax year (e.g., taxpayers who marry or divorce). The final regulation acknowledges that certain circumstances may make filing jointly a challenge (e.g., domestic abuse, abandonment, etc.); it states that the IRS will propose additional rules to address these kinds of circumstances.

Enrolled in an Individual Exchange

Premium credits are available only to individuals and families enrolled in a plan offered through an individual exchange; premium credits are *not* available through the small business (SHOP) exchanges. Individuals may enroll in a plan through their state's exchange if they are (1) residing in a state in which an exchange was established; (2) not incarcerated, except individuals in custody pending the disposition of charges; and (3) "lawfully present" residents.[20]

Only lawful residents are allowed to obtain exchange coverage. Undocumented individuals are prohibited from purchasing coverage through an exchange, even if they could pay the entire premium without a subsidy.[21] Because the ACA prohibits undocumented individuals from obtaining exchange coverage, they are *not* eligible for premium credits.

The final regulation clarifies the potential credit eligibility for family members of individuals who themselves are *not* eligible to enroll in an exchange due to incarceration or legal status. For example, while the final regulation restates the ACA's prohibition on incarcerated individuals enrolling in exchange plans, the rule confirms that family members (of incarcerated individuals) who enroll in exchange plans may receive premium credits, as long as the family members meet all eligibility criteria.[22]

Household Income Is 100%-400% of Federal Poverty Level

Individuals generally must have household income within statutorily defined guidelines (based on the federal poverty level [FPL][23]) to be eligible for premium credits, with some exceptions. For purposes of premium credit eligibility, household income is measured according to the definition for modified adjusted gross income (MAGI).[24] An individual whose MAGI is at or above 100% FPL up to and including 400% FPL may be eligible to receive premium credits.[25]

Table 1 displays the income levels at 400% FPL, the amount *beyond* which individuals and families would *not* be eligible for premium credits in 2015 (using 2014 HHS poverty guidelines).[26]

Table 1. Income Levels at 400% FPL Applicable to 2015 Premium Credit Eligibility (based on 2014 HHS poverty guidelines)

Number of Persons in Family	48 Contiguous States and DC	Alaska	Hawaii
1	$46,680	$58,320	$53,680
2	$62,920	$78,640	$72,360
3	$79,160	$98,960	$91,040
4	$95,400	$119,280	$109,720
5	$111,640	$139,600	$128,400
6	$127,880	$159,920	$147,080
7	$144,120	$180,240	$165,760
8	$160,360	$200,560	$184,440

Source: Congressional Research Service computations based on "Annual Update of the HHS Poverty Guidelines," 79 Federal Register 3593, January 22, 2014, http://www.gpo.gov/fdsys/pkg/FR-2014-01-22/pdf/2014- 01303.pdf.

Notes: For 2015, the income levels used to calculate premium credit eligibility and amounts are based on 2014 Department of Health and Human Services (HHS) poverty guidelines. The poverty guidelines are updated annually for inflation. FPL = federal poverty level; DC = District of Columbia.

Not Eligible for "Minimum Essential Coverage"

To receive a premium credit, an individual may *not* be *eligible* for "minimum essential coverage," with exceptions (described below). The ACA broadly defines minimum essential coverage to include Medicare Part A; Medicare Advantage; Medicaid (with exceptions); the State Children's Health Insurance Program (CHIP); Tricare; Tricare for Life, a health care program administered by the Department of Veterans Affairs (VA);[27] the Peace Corps program; any government plan (local, state, federal) including the Federal Employees Health Benefits Program (FEHBP); any plan offered in the individual health insurance market; any employer-sponsored plan (including group plans regulated by a foreign government); any grandfathered health plan;[28] any qualified health plan offered inside or outside of exchanges; and any other coverage (such as a state high risk pool) recognized by the HHS Secretary.[29]

Exceptions to Minimum Essential Coverage Eligibility

The ACA provides certain exceptions regarding eligibility for minimum essential coverage and receipt of premium credits:

- An individual who is only eligible to obtain coverage through the individual (nongroup) health insurance market30 may be eligible to receive a premium credit.
- An individual eligible for an employer-sponsored plan may still be eligible for premium credits if the employer's coverage is either (1) not affordable; that is, the employee's premium contribution toward the employer's self-only plan exceeds 9.56% of household income;[31] or (2) does not provide minimum value; that is, the plan's payments cover less than 60% of total allowed costs on average.[32]
- An individual who is eligible for limited benefits under Medicaid may still be eligible for premium credits (see "Medicaid" section below for additional information).

Employer Contribution Toward Coverage in SHOP Exchanges

Certain small employers (and in later years, large employers at state option) may offer and contribute toward coverage through SHOP exchanges. If an individual is enrolled in an exchange through an employer who contributed toward that coverage, the individual will *not* be eligible for premium credits.[33]

Medicaid

The ACA's Medicaid expansion provisions have the potential for affecting eligibility for premium credits if certain low to middle income individuals and families seek health insurance through the exchanges.[34] Under the ACA, states have the option to expand Medicaid eligibility to include all non-elderly, non-pregnant individuals (i.e., childless adults and certain parents, except for those ineligible based on certain non-citizenship status) with income up to 138% FPL.[35] (The ACA does not change noncitizens' eligibility for Medicaid.[36]) States that have chosen to implement the ACA Medicaid expansion have received substantial federal subsidies. If a person who applied for premium credits in an exchange is determined to be eligible for Medicaid, the exchange must have them enrolled in Medicaid.[37] Therefore, in states that have expanded Medicaid eligibility to include persons with incomes at or above 100% FPL (or any state that currently includes such individuals), premium credit eligibility begins at the income level where Medicaid eligibility ends.

In general, a person may be eligible for only one subsidized health coverage program at a time. However, exceptions are made for individuals who are eligible only for limited benefits under Medicaid; limited benefits include the pregnancy-related benefits package, treatment of emergency medical conditions only, and other limited benefits. Individuals who have access to specified limited benefits under Medicaid may qualify for premium credits if such individuals enroll in exchanges.[38]

Required Premium Contributions and Premium Credit Calculations

The amount of the premium tax credit varies from person to person; the credit is based on the household income of the tax filer (and dependents), the premium for the exchange plan in which the tax filer (and dependents) is (are) enrolled, and other factors. In certain instances, the credit amount may cover the entire premium and the tax filer pays nothing toward the premium. In other instances, the tax filer may pay part (or all)[39] of the premium.

The credit amount is based on a comparison of two amounts that result from two different scenarios. The first scenario (and amount) is straightforward: the premium for the exchange plan in which the person/family enrolls. The second scenario is more complicated, involving a formula that considers the premium for a reference plan in the local area in which the person/family resides, and an amount that the person/family may be required to contribute toward the premium. Based on a comparison of the amounts resulting from each scenario, the premium credit will be the lesser amount. The following text box, "Calculation of the Premium Credit Amount," discusses these two scenarios in more detail.

Calculation of the Premium Credit Amount

The premium credit amount will be the lesser amount resulting from either:

Scenario A: The cost of the exchange plan that the tax filer (and dependents) is (are) enrolled in;

Or

Scenario B: The excess, if any, resulting from the following formula:

The age-adjusted premium for the second-lowest-cost silver plan in the tax filer's area (reference plan),

Minus

The product of the tax filer's household income and the applicable percentage (explained in greater detail below), based on the tax filer's household income relative to the federal poverty level.

Enrollee Premium Contribution

The enrollee premium contribution will be based on the lesser amount calculated above.

Scenario A: If the premium credit is based on the amount calculated under Scenario A, then the tax filer (and dependents) pay(s) nothing toward the premium for exchange coverage.

Scenario B: If the premium credit is based on the amount calculated under Scenario B, then the tax filer (and dependents) pay(s) some amount toward the premium for exchange coverage.

Choice of Exchange Plan Enrollment

While the calculation in Scenario B is based on the second-lowest-cost silver plan in the tax filer's local area, the qualifying individual/family may enroll in any tiered plan in an exchange and still be eligible for a tax credit. However, if the individual/family enrolls in a plan with a premium that exceeds the premium for the reference plan, the individual/family is responsible for paying that additional amount.

Under Scenario B, the amount that a tax filer who receives a premium credit is required to contribute toward the premium (for the reference plan) is capped as a percentage of household income; that is, the *maximum premium contribution* is the product of the tax filer's household income and the "applicable percentage," as specified in the ACA. In general, the applicable percentage is less for those with lower incomes compared with those with higher incomes; where income is measured relative to the federal poverty level. Under Scenario B, the amount that tax filers with income between 100% FPL and 133% FPL may be required to contribute toward the reference plan's premium is capped at 2.01% of household income for 2015. For tax filers with income 300%-400% FPL, their premium contribution is capped at 9.56% of income. The IRS further specifies the applicable percentages, for tax filers whose incomes are between those two income bands[40] (see *Figure 1*).

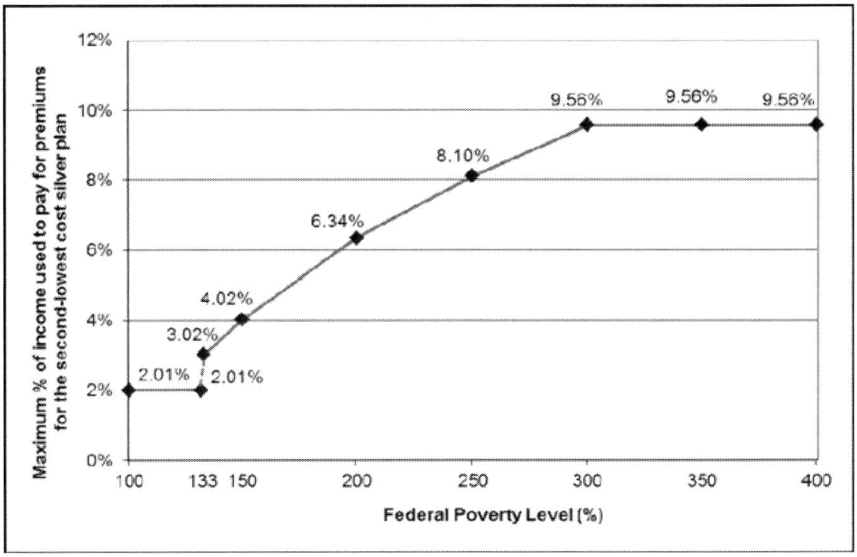

Source: IRS Revenue Procedure 2014-37, http://www.irs.gov/pub/irs-drop/rp-14-37.pdf.

Note: The Patient Protection and Affordable Care Act (ACA) statute specifies the maximum percentages of income, as measured relative to the federal poverty level (FPL), to calculate the tax filer's required premium contribution. The ACA specified the "applicable percentages" at the following FPLs: 133%, 150%, 200%, 250%, 300%, and 400%. The percentages jump at 133% FPL; the dotted line in the graph illustrates the cliff effect of the statutory requirements.

Figure 1. Maximum Percentage of Household Income to Go Toward 2015 Premiums for the Second-Lowes Cost Silver Plan, by Percentage of the Federal Poverty Level. (applicable to premium tax credit recipients).

The line graph shows the "applicable percentage" used to calculate the tax filer's required premium contribution at each income level, as measured relative to the federal poverty level. The ACA statute specifies the applicable percentage at certain incomes (income at 100% FPL, 133% FPL, 150% FPL, etc.) beginning in 2014 and indexed in later years. At each of those incomes, the line changes slope. Specifically, at and above 133% FPL up to 300% FPL, the applicable percentage increases *incrementally* as income increases. For example, a person with income at 150% FPL may be required to pay a maximum of 4.02% of household income toward exchange coverage in the reference plan. A 1% increase in income (i.e., person has income at 151% FPL) results in a maximum premium contribution equal to 4.07% of income.[41] In contrast to this gradual change in the maximum premium contribution for incomes between 133% and 300% FPL, there is a "cliff" for a person/family with income below 133% FPL. Instead of the incremental change discussed above, the contribution amount jumps when you compare income just *below* 133% FPL with income *at* 133% FPL. This cliff reflects statutory requirements.[42]

Given that calculation of the premium credit amount (under Scenario B) is the arithmetic difference after subtracting the tax filer's required premium contribution from the premium for the second-lowest-cost silver plan (reference plan), it is theoretically possible that a person's required premium contribution could be equal to or exceed the reference plan's premium. Such a scenario would leave that tax filer with a premium credit of zero.43 Moreover, while the credit amount under this scenario is based on the reference plan, the individual/family may enroll in any metal-tier plan and still be eligible for credits. However, when a premium credit recipient enrolls in a plan that is more expensive than the reference plan, that person must pay the additional premium amount.

PREMIUM CREDITS IN 2015

For 2015, *Table 2* displays selected annual income levels used in the calculation of premium credit amounts and required premium contributions, as discussed above.

Table 2. Selected Annual Income Levels Applicable to 2015 Premium Credits (based on 2014 HHS poverty guidelines for the 48 contiguous states and the District of Columbia)

Percentage of Federal			Family Size	
Poverty Line (FPL)	1 person	2 persons	3 persons	4 persons
100%	$11,670	$15,730	$19,790	$23,850
Poverty Line (FPL)	1 person	2 persons	3 persons	4 persons
133%	$15,521	$20,921	$26,321	$31,721
150%	$17,505	$23,595	$29,685	$35,775
200%	$23,340	$31,460	$39,580	$47,700
250%	$29,175	$39,325	$49,475	$59,625
300%	$35,010	$47,190	$59,370	$71,550
350%	$40,845	$55,055	$69,265	$83,475
400%	$46,680	$62,920	$79,160	$95,400

Source: CRS computations based on "Annual Update of the HHS Poverty Guidelines," 79 Federal Register 3593, January 22, 2014, http://www.gpo.gov/fdsys/pkg/FR-2014-01-22/pdf/2014-01303.pdf.

Notes: For 2015, the income levels used to calculate premium credit eligibility and amounts are based on 2014 Department of Health and Human Services (HHS) poverty guidelines. Different income levels, as measured against the federal poverty level, apply separately to Alaska and Hawaii (see Table 1).

Table 3 displays the maximum *monthly* premium contributions for individuals and families who receive premium tax credits, provided that they enroll in the applicable reference plan.

Both *Figure 1* and *Table 3* illustrate the cliff effect that occurs at 133% FPL. For individuals with income *below* 133% FPL, the credit formula ensures that such individuals pay no more than 2.01% of their income for the second-lowest-cost silver plan. For incomes *at* 133% FPL, individuals and families may pay 3.02% of their income toward premiums for the reference plan. For example, an individual with income at 132.99% FPL (annual income of $15,520) may be required to pay $26 in monthly premiums for the second-lowest-cost plan in 2015 (see *Table 3*). With one additional dollar of income (annual income of $15,521, equivalent to 133% FPL), this person may be required to pay $39 in monthly premiums. Therefore, the additional $1 in annual income may lead to an additional $156 in premium contributions for this hypothetical person in 2015. Nevertheless, some might observe that prior to implementation of the ACA premium credits in 2014, there were no federal subsidies for health coverage for individuals with income at this level and above, except for some narrowly defined groups. Thus, more individuals overall may be eligible for subsidized private coverage under the ACA, than before enactment of the law.

Table 3. Maximum Monthly Premium Contributions for Tax Credit Recipients Enrolled in the Second-Lowest-Cost Silver Plan, by Income, 2015 (based on 2014 HHS poverty guidelines for the 48 contiguous states and the District of Columbia)

Federal Poverty Line (FPL)	Maximum Premium Contribution based on a Percentage of Income (Applicable Percentages)	1 person	2 persons	3 persons	4 persons
100%	2.01%	$20	$26	$33	$40
132.99%	2.01%	$26	$35	$44	$53
133%	3.02%	$39	$53	$66	$80
150%	4.02%	$59	$79	$99	$120
200%	6.34%	$123	$166	$209	$252
250%	8.10%	$197	$265	$334	$402
300%	9.56%	$279	$376	$473	$570
350%	9.56%	$325	$439	$552	$665
400%	9.56%	$372	$501	$631	$760

Source: CRS computations based on "Annual Update of the HHS Poverty Guidelines," 79 Federal Register 3593, January 22, 2014, http://www.gpo.gov/fdsys/pkg/FR-2014-01-22/pdf/2014-01303.pdf.

Notes: For 2015, the income levels used to calculate premium credit eligibility and amounts are based on 2014 Department of Health and Human Services (HHS) poverty guidelines. If individuals enroll in more expensive plans than the second-lowest-cost silver plan in their respective areas, they would be responsible for the additional premium amounts. If the required premium contribution exceeds the actual premium amount, individuals would pay the entire premium for exchange coverage. The premium contributions have been rounded up to the nearest dollar amount.

Premium Credit Examples: Self-Only and Family Coverage

The following hypothetical examples use actual exchange information about premiums, enrollee contributions, and estimated premium credit amounts; the information was compiled using the plan finder tool at healthcare.gov.[44] To facilitate comparisons across hypothetical individuals and families, the premium and estimated tax credit amounts apply to the same zip code: 60647 (the same zip code used as an example in the plan finder tool at https://www.healthcare.gov/see-plans/). The examples in *Table 4* assume that the hypothetical individual (or family) is enrolled in the reference plan (second-lowest-cost silver plan). As the 2015 premium data indicate, individuals at the same income level will face different (pre-credit) premiums based on age. This reflects the limited age rating allowed for health insurance policies, including those offered in the individual exchanges.[45] The practical effect of the ACA's age rating requirements means that, for any given metal-tier plan in a specific geographic area, premiums vary for adults between 21 and 64+ years of age by a 3:1 ratio. (For examples that illustrate the 3:1 ratio for adults, see hypothetical persons A, B, C, and D in *Table 4* and the following analysis included under "Discussion of Self-Only Coverage Examples.") Moreover, the premium credit amounts are greater for those with lower incomes, compared with higher-income individuals of the same age, reflecting the income-based structure of the premium credits.

Discussion of Self-Only Coverage Examples

As indicated *Table 4* the monthly (pre-credit) premiums for self-only coverage in the secondlowest-cost silver plan in zip code: 60647, are $168 for a 21-year-old individual and $506 for a 64-year-old individual.[46] Given the 3:1 age-rating among adults between 21 and 64+ years of age, it follows that the premium for the same plan in the same county is approximately three times greater for the older adults (hypothetical persons B and D), than it is for the younger adults (hypothetical persons A and C). That is, hypothetical persons A and C (both of whom are 21 years of age) have a pre-credit premium of $168, compared to hypothetical persons B and D (both of whom are 64 years of age) who have a pre-credit premium of $506.

However, for premium credit recipients, age does *not* determine the amount that a given person contributes toward the premium. The formula for calculating premium contributions from enrollees is based on income (see *Table 3*), and such contributions are calculated prior to determining the credit amount. Therefore, the actual amount that tax credit recipients will pay toward exchange premiums may be the same for individuals with the same income levels, regardless of age. For example, persons A and B are very different in age but have the same income level; therefore, their required monthly contributions toward premiums are the same amount ($59). Person C is an example of the exception to this general rule. Persons C and D have the same

[b] The premiums for the plans that are currently being offered through exchanges vary according to metal tier, geographic location, family size, age, and other factors.

[c] The maximum premium contribution for an individual whose income is $40,845 in 2015 is approximately $325 per month. However, the monthly premium in this example is $168, which is a lower amount than the maximum premium contribution for the second-lowest-cost silver plan. Given this, hypothetical person C pays the entire premium for coverage in this plan, and the credit amount is zero.

[d] Premiums for exchange plans are allowed to vary based on family size. In this table, hypothetical families E through H are each composed of two adults of the same age and one child who is age 19. Insurance rates for children are calculated by considering individuals under age 21 as one group. For example, if one child who is age 5 and another child who is age 19 enrolled in the same metal-tier plan, their (pre-credit) premiums would be the same amount.

[e] The maximum premium contribution for a family of three whose income is $69,265 in 2015 is approximately $552 per month. However, the monthly premium in this example is $538, which is a lower amount than the maximum premium contribution for the second-lowest-cost silver plan. Given this, hypothetical family G pays the entire premium for coverage in this plan and the credit amount is zero.

They will have to repay the excess when they file federal income taxes for that year. However, if such a family has income below 200% FPL, the IRS may only require them to repay up to $600 (for tax credit overpayments during that tax year). In other words, while such a family may technically owe a larger amount, repayment is limited to a maximum of $600 for a family with income below 200% FPL.

Table 5. Limits on Repayment of Excess Premium Credits Enacted by the Comprehensive 1099 Taxpayer Protection and Repayment of Exchange Subsidy Overpayment Act of 2011 (P.L. 112-9)

If Household Income (Expressed as a Percentage of the Federal Poverty Level) Is	Then the Applicable Dollar Limit for Joint Filers Is
Less than 200%	$600
At least 200% but less than 300%	$1,500
At least 300% but less than 400%	$2,500

Note: The applicable dollar limit for single filers is 50% of the joint-filer limit.

Limited Tax Relief for Certain Premium Credit Recipients

On January 26, 2015, the IRS announced that premium credit recipients who owe a payment on their 2014 tax return, as a result of the tax credit reconciliation process, may receive limited tax relief.[49] For the 2014 tax year only, taxpayers who meet specified eligibility criteria will be given relief from penalties related to the following scenarios: (1) late payment of taxes owed[50] and (2) underpayment of taxes owed.[51] In other words, this relief for 2014 only applies to penalties related to late payment or underpayment of taxes; the relief does not negate the taxpayer's obligation to pay back excess premium credit amounts calculated under the reconciliation process. Moreover, this limited relief does not provide taxpayers with an extension to file their return, nor does it provide relief from any underpayment related to the penalty for not complying with the ACA's individual mandate.[52]

To qualify for penalty relief under the first scenario, taxpayers must otherwise be in compliance with other tax filing and payment requirements; owe a tax payment as a result of premium credit overpayments that were advanced during the 2014 tax year; and report the excess amount of advanced credit payments on their timely filed 2014 tax return. To qualify for penalty relief under the second scenario, taxpayers must otherwise be in compliance with other tax filing and payment requirements and report the excess amount of advanced credit payments on their timely filed 2014 tax return.

EXCHANGE PLAN SELECTION AND PREMIUM CREDITS

On March 10, 2015, HHS announced that nearly 11.7 million persons selected a metal plan through the individual exchanges, with 86% determined to be eligible for premium tax credits.[53]

These data reflect exchange plan selections through the standard open enrollment period as well as the special enrollment period (SEP) that ended on February 22, 2015.[54]

For 2015 exchange enrollment, HHS is providing another special enrollment period. This SEP is for individuals residing in states in which the federal government administers the exchanges who were uninsured in 2014 and are subject to the penalty for noncompliance with the individual mandate. Individuals who meet the requirements specified in the SEP announcement[55] will be allowed to enroll in an exchange plan during the SEP (March 15, 2015, through April 30, 2015).

In its past and current estimates of the ACA's health coverage provisions, the Congressional Budget Office (CBO) projects exchange enrollment to be modest in the first few years, then increase significantly afterwards. Likewise, the estimates of federal outlays for premium credits are relatively moderate initially, but increase rapidly after the first few years. According to its latest estimates, CBO projects exchange enrollment in 2015 to total 12 million persons: 11 million and 1 million persons enrolled in the individual and SHOP exchanges, respectively. By 2025, CBO estimates that 25 million individuals will be enrolled in exchange coverage. Of those exchange enrollees who are enrolled in the individual exchanges (22 million), 16 million are projected to receive premium credits (see *Figure 2*). CBO estimates that federal outlays for premium credits will total $599 billion from FY2016 through FY2025.[56]

COST-SHARING SUBSIDIES

In addition to the premium credits, the ACA established subsidies that are applicable to cost-sharing expenses. An individual who qualifies for the premium credit *and* is enrolled in a silver plan (actuarial value of 70%)

through an exchange is also eligible for cost-sharing assistance.[57] The assistance is provided in two forms, and both forms are based on income (see descriptions below). Individuals who receive cost-sharing subsidies may receive both types, as long as they meet the applicable eligibility requirements.

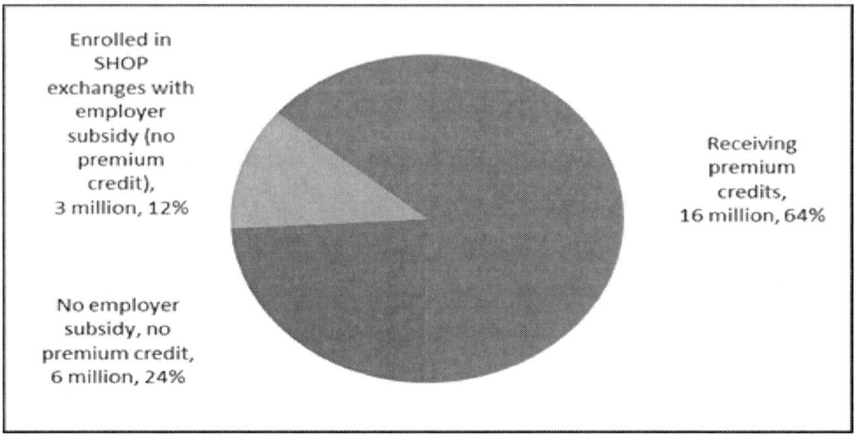

Source: U.S. Congressional Budget Office, "Insurance Coverage Provisions of the Affordable Care Act—CBO's March 2015 Baseline," March 2015, http://www.cbo.gov/sites/default/files/cbofiles/attachments/43900-2015-03-ACAtables.pdf.

Notes: The estimate for individuals receiving premium credits includes individuals who were determined to be eligible for such credits because their employer plan was either unaffordable or did not provide minimum value ("inadequate"), per the ACA statute. The latest CBO projections for the ACA's insurance coverage provisions estimated that individuals with unaffordable or inadequate employer coverage was less than 1 million total; therefore, counts for those individuals were not published separately from other individuals who received premium credits through the standard eligibility process.

Figure 2. Total Estimated Exchange Enrollment, 2025.

The ACA requires each metal tier plan to limit the total amount an enrollee will be required to pay out of pocket for use of covered services in a year (referred to as an annual cost-sharing limit in this report), and establishes separate limits for self-only coverage and family coverage. For 2015, the annual cost-sharing limit for self-only coverage is $6,450; the corresponding limit for family coverage is $12,900.[58] Given that tiered plans will already be required to comply with those annual cost-sharing limits, one form of cost-sharing assistance reduces such limits (see *Table 6*). The cost-sharing assistance reduces the annual limit faced by eligible individuals with income between 100% and 250% FPL; greater reductions are provided to those with lower incomes. In general, this cost-sharing assistance targets individuals and families who use a great deal of health care in a year and, therefore, have high cost-sharing expenses. Enrollees who use very little health care do not generate enough cost-sharing expenses to reach the annual limit.

Table 6. ACA Cost-Sharing Subsidies: Annual Cost-Sharing Limits, by Household Income Tier, 2015

Household Income Tier, by Federal Poverty Level	Annual Cost-Sharing Limits	
	Self-Only Coverage	Family Coverage
100% - 150%	$2,250	$4,500
Greater than 150% - 200%	$2,250	$4,500
Greater than 200% - 250%	$5,200	$10,400

Source: "HHS Notice of Benefit and Payment Parameters for 2015," 79 Federal Register 13744, March 11, 2014, http://www.gpo.gov/fdsys/pkg/FR-2014-03-11/pdf/2-14-05052.pdf.

Note: The cost-sharing limits applicable to tiered plans established under the ACA use existing limits applicable to high-deductible health plans (HDHPs) that qualify to be paired with health savings accounts (HSAs). For 2015, the cost-sharing limits for HSA-qualified HDHPs are $6,450 for self-only coverage, and $12,900 for family coverage. The cost-sharing subsidy reduces these annual limits based on income.

The second form of cost-sharing assistance also applies to individuals with income between 100% and 250% FPL. For eligible individuals, the cost-sharing requirements (in the plans they have enrolled) have been reduced to ensure that the plan covers a certain percentage of allowed health care expenses, on average. The practical effect of this cost-sharing assistance is to increase the actuarial value (AV)[59] of the exchange plan in which the person is enrolled (*Table 7*), so enrollees face lower cost-sharing requirements than they would have without this assistance. Given that this form of cost-sharing assistance directly affects cost-sharing requirements (e.g., lower deductible), both enrollees who use minimal health care and those who use a great deal of services may potentially benefit from this assistance.

Table 7. ACA Cost-Sharing Subsidies: Actuarial Values, by Household Income Tier

Household Income Tier, by Federal Poverty Level	New Actuarial Values for Cost-Sharing Subsidy Recipients
100%-150%	94%
Greater than 150%-200%	87%
Greater than 200%-250%	73%

Source: 45 C.F.R. §156.420.

To be eligible for cost-sharing subsidies, an individual must be enrolled in a silver plan, so that coverage already has an AV of 70%. For an individual who receives the subsidy referred to in *Table 7*, the health plan imposes a set of different cost-sharing requirements, so the "silver" plan will meet the new applicable AV. The ACA statute does not specify how a plan reduces cost-sharing requirements to increase the AV from 70% to one of the higher AVs. Through regulations, HHS requires each insurance company that offers a plan that is subject to these cost-sharing reductions to develop variations of its silver plan; these silver plan variations must comply with the higher levels of actuarial value (73%, 87%, and 94%).[60] When an individual is determined by an exchange to be eligible for a cost-sharing subsidy, the person is enrolled in the plan variation that corresponds with that person's income (as indicated in *Table 7*). This approach allows an individual to benefit automatically from this type of assistance, as soon as he or she uses health care that is covered under the exchange plan.

The HHS Secretary will provide full reimbursements to exchange plans that provide cost-sharing subsidies.[61] A given health plan is required to submit to HHS estimates of the amount of cost-sharing assistance it will provide in a year. Such estimates must be submitted prior to that year to receive advance payments for the estimated amount of cost-sharing assistance. A plan also must submit to HHS actual amounts of cost-sharing assistance provided. The actual amounts will be periodically reconciled with the amounts received by the plan in advance payments.[62] CBO estimates that federal outlays for the cost-sharing subsidies will total $136 billion from FY2016 through FY2025.[63]

End Notes

[1] §1401 of the Patient Protection and Affordable Care Act (ACA; P.L. 111-148, as amended), new §36B of the Internal Revenue Code of 1986 (IRC).

[2] For information about types of exchanges, see Kaiser Family Foundation, "State Health Insurance Marketplace Types, 2015," at http://kff.org/health-reform/state-indicator/state-health-insurance-marketplace-types/.

[3] Enrollment in an exchange plan is voluntary; see §1312(d)(3) of the ACA. This also applies to Members of Congress and their personal staff who may only be offered coverage by the federal government that is created under the ACA or offered through an exchange, per the ACA §1312(d)(3)(D). Although the federal government may make only certain plans available to applicable Members and staff, such individuals may enroll in any plan that is available to them. For a comprehensive discussion about these issues, see CRS Report R43194, Health Benefits for Members of Congress and Certain Congressional Staff.

[4] Before 2016, states will have the option to define small employers either as those with (1) 100 or fewer employees, or (2) 50 or fewer employees. Beginning in 2016, small employers will be defined as those with 100 or fewer employees. Beginning in 2017, large groups may participate in exchanges, at state option.

[5] See CRS Report R42069, Private Health Insurance Market Reforms in the Affordable Care Act (ACA).

[6] Actuarial value (AV) is a summary measure of a plan's generosity, expressed as the percentage of medical expenses estimated to be paid by the insurer for a standard population and set of allowed charges. AV is not a measure of premiums or the benefits package. Two plans with the same AV may have different premiums and different sets of covered benefits.

[7] Since actuarial value is calculated based on a population, this measure indicates plan generosity for a group. It does not indicate the share of medical expenses that the plan will pay for each individual enrolled in a plan. The utility of AV is that it facilitates comparisons across plans, so that an individual/family may use this plan characteristic (along with other factors) to decide on the most appropriate plan given anticipated health care needs and disposable income.

[8] See CRS Report R43771, Small Business Health Options Program (SHOP) Exchange.

[9] The ACA statute does not specify the features of such an exchange, except that the exchange must have "adequate resources" to provide assistance to both types of customers. See §1401(b)(2) of the ACA.

[10] For tax years beginning after December 31, 2013, 31 U.S.C. 1324 appropriates necessary amounts to the Treasury Secretary for disbursements due under §36B of the IRC. This permanent appropriation means that the premium credits do not require annual appropriations.

[11] The formula for calculating the premium credit amount is such that it is possible for a higher-income person who is technically eligible for a credit to end up receiving no credit to offset the cost of buying insurance. For additional information about this issue, see the discussion under the "Required Premium Contributions and Premium Credit Calculations" section of this report.

[12] 77 Federal Register 30377, May 23, 2012.

[13] See the IRS's "Affordable Care Act (ACA) Tax Provisions" webpage for links to such documents at http://www.irs.gov/Affordable-Care-Act.

[14] 759 F.3d 358, (4th Cir. 2014), cert. granted, 83 U.S.L.W. 3286 (U.S. November 7, 2014) (No. 14-114).

[15] §1401(a) of the ACA, new §36B(c)(1) of the IRC.

[16] The guidelines that designate the federal poverty level are used in a variety of federal programs for eligibility purposes. The poverty guidelines vary by family size, and by whether the individual resides in the 48 contiguous states and the District of Columbia, Alaska, or

Hawaii. Office of the Assistant Secretary for Planning and Evaluation, "Frequently Asked Questions Related to the Poverty Guidelines and Poverty," http://aspe.hhs.gov/Poverty/faq.cfm#programs.

[17] Consumers Union's Tax Credit Brochures are available to help tax filers determine their eligibility for premium tax credits. See "Cut the Cost of Health Insurance," http://www.consumersunion.org/tax_credit_brochure.

[18] As specified under §1412(a)(3) of the ACA, advanced credits are provided from the Treasury Department to insurers. The Department of Health and Human Services (HHS) provides payment information to Treasury. Treasury then processes the Electronic File Transfer and sends credit payments directly to the insurer's financial institution. See FAQs 463 and 500, https://www.regtap.info/.

[19] On June 26, 2013, in United States v. Windsor, the U.S. Supreme Court struck down Section 3 of the Defense of Marriage Act (DOMA), finding that it violated the equal protection guarantees of the Fifth Amendment. Section 3 had required that, for purposes of federal enactments, marriage be defined as the union of one man and one woman. In light of this ruling, HHS issued guidance which stated that same-sex spouses will be treated just like opposite-sex spouses for premium credit eligibility purposes. See Centers for Medicare & Medicaid Services, "Guidance on Internal Revenue Ruling 2013-17 and Eligibility for Advance Payments of the Premium Tax Credit and Cost-Sharing Reductions," Sept. 27, 2013, http://www.cms.gov/CCIIO/Resources/Regulations-and-Guidance/Downloads/marketplace-guidance-on-irs-2013-17.pdf.

[20] §1401(a) of the ACA, new §36B of the IRC.

[21] §1312(f)(3) of the ACA.

[22] See discussion under "Individuals not lawfully present or incarcerated," 77 Federal Register 30377, May 23, 2012.

[23] The poverty guidelines are updated annually, at the beginning of the year. However, premium credit calculations are based on the prior year's guidelines to provide individuals with timely information as they compare and enroll in exchange plans during the open enrollment period (which occurs prior to the beginning of the plan year). For the poverty guidelines used to calculate the credit amounts for 2015, see "Annual Update of the HHS Poverty Guidelines," 79 Federal Register 3593, January 22, 2014, http://www.gpo.gov/fdsys/pkg/FR-2014-01-22/pdf/2014-01303.pdf.

[24] In §2002(a) and §1401(a) of the ACA, household income is defined to be MAGI, in compliance with the Internal Revenue Code (IRC). Under the IRC, gross income is total income minus certain exclusions (e.g., public assistance payments, employer contributions to health insurance payments). From gross income, adjusted gross income (AGI) is calculated to reflect a number of deductions, including trade and business deductions, losses from sale of property, and alimony payments. MAGI is defined as AGI plus certain foreign earned income and tax-exempt interest. However, for premium credit eligibility purposes, the definition of MAGI will also include nontaxable Social Security benefits (as amended by P.L. 112-56). For additional discussion about the use of MAGI with respect to the ACA premium credits, see CRS Report R43861, The Use of Modified Adjusted Gross Income (MAGI) in Federal Health Programs.

[25] There are exceptions to the lower bound income threshold at 100% FPL. One exception relates to the state option under the ACA to expand Medicaid for individuals with income up to 133% FPL (with a 5% income disregard). If a state chooses to undertake the ACA Medicaid expansion (or has already expanded Medicaid above 100% FPL), eligibility for premium credits would begin above the income level where Medicaid eligibility ends in such a state.

(Note that in states that do not expand Medicaid to at least 100% FPL, some low-income state residents are ineligible for both premium credits and Medicaid.) Another exception is for lawfully present aliens with income below 100% FPL, who are not eligible for Medicaid for the first five years that they are lawfully present. The ACA established section 36B(c)(1)(B) of the IRC to allow such lawfully present aliens to still be eligible for premium credits. Likewise, the final regulation on premium credits provided a special rule for credit recipients whose income at the end of the tax year end up being less than 100% FPL. Such individuals will continue to be considered "applicable taxpayers" for premium credit eligibility purposes. For regulatory language applicable to lawfully present aliens and individuals whose incomes are below 100% FPL at the end of the tax year, see 26 C.F.R. 1.36B-2(b)(5), (6), and (7).

[26] See Internal Revenue Service, "Questions and Answers on the Premium Tax Credit," Q&A #6, http://www.irs.gov/uac/Newsroom/Questions-and-Answers-on-the-Premium-Tax-Credit.

[27] The IRS final regulation on premium credits stated that for premium credit eligibility purposes, a person would be considered "eligible" for a VA health program only if that person is actually enrolled in such a program. Therefore, individuals who could enroll in such programs, but choose not to enroll, may be eligible for premium credits, providing they meet all other eligibility criteria. See discussion under "Special rule for coverage for veterans and other individuals under chapter 17 or 18 of Title 38, U.S.C.," 77 Federal Register 30377, May 23, 2012.

[28] A grandfathered health plan is a group health plan or health insurance coverage (including coverage from the individual health insurance market) in which a person was enrolled since the date of enactment of the ACA. For additional information about grandfathered plans, see CRS Report R41166, Grandfathered Health Plans Under the Patient Protection and Affordable Care Act (ACA).

[29] The IRS final regulation on premium credits addresses various circumstances when individuals transition between exchange coverage and public coverage, such as Medicaid. For example, the regulation discusses the process and time period applicable to an individual who becomes eligible for "government-sponsored coverage," and therefore becomes ineligible for premium credits. See discussion under "Government-Sponsored Coverage" and "Determination of Medicaid or Children's Health Insurance Program (CHIP)," 77 Federal Register 30377, May 23, 2012.

[30] The private health insurance market continues to exist outside of the ACA exchanges. Moreover, almost all exchange plans are allowed to be offered in the market outside of exchanges.

[31] The IRS final regulation on premium credits confirms that an employee safe harbor will be provided to an individual who initially is determined to be eligible for premium credits because the employer plan is unaffordable to that individual, but later in the year the individual has access to an affordable employer plan and technically is not eligible for credits. The employee safe harbor allows such individuals to continue to be eligible for credits for the rest of the year. Moreover, the employer would not be subject to a penalty because a full-time employee receives a premium credit under the safe harbor.

[32] §1401(a) of the ACA, new §36B(c)(2)(C) of the IRC.

[33] §1401(a) of the ACA, new §36B(c)(2)(A)(ii) of the IRC.

[34] See CRS Report R43564, The ACA Medicaid Expansion.

[35] The ACA specifies that the Medicaid expansion increases eligibility for individuals with incomes up to 133% FPL, with an income disregard of 5%. Thus, the effective minimum

income eligibility threshold for such individuals in this new Medicaid eligibility group will be 138% FPL.

[36] As under law prior to the ACA, certain lawfully present aliens are eligible for full Medicaid benefits (e.g., refugees, asylees, and some legal permanent residents [LPRs] who have been here at least five years), whereas others are not (e.g., certain LPRs who have been here less than five years).

[37] §§1311(d)(4) and 1413(a) of the ACA. Nonetheless, nothing in the ACA prohibits a Medicaid-eligible individual from enrolling in an exchange on his/her own. However, that individual will be responsible for the entire cost of exchange coverage, which will likely be prohibitive for a low-income individual.

[38] See Health Reform GPS, "When Does Medicaid Coverage Amount to Minimum Essential Coverage Under the Affordable Care Act? An Update on the Treasury/IRS Rules Defining Minimum Essential Coverage," February 11, 2014, http://www.healthreformgps.org/resources/when-does-medicaid-coverage-amount-to-minimum-essentialcoverage-under-the-affordable-care-act-an-update-on-the-treasuryirs-rules-defining-minimum-essential-coverage/.

[39] The formula for calculating the premium credit amount is such that it is possible that the result may be a credit of zero dollars, meaning the person/family pays the entire exchange premium. See the text box "Calculation of the Premium Credit Amount" for additional information.

[40] See IRS Revenue Procedure 2014-37, http://www.irs.gov/pub/irs-drop/rp-14-37.pdf.

[41] The formula to calculate "applicable percentages" is discussed in 26 C.F.R. 1.36B-3.

[42] See the ACA, §1401(a), new §36B(b)(3)(A) of the IRC; and 26 C.F.R. 1.36B-3.

[43] For an illustrative example, see hypothetical person "C" and table note "c" in Table 4 of this report.

[44] To find local plan information, premiums, and estimated tax credit amounts in federally facilitated exchanges (no registration necessary), see https://www.healthcare.gov/see-plans/. Residents in states with state-based exchanges may go directly to such exchanges, or can input a zip code at https://www.healthcare.gov/see-plans/ and be redirected to the relevant state-based exchange website.

[45] For additional information about age rating under the ACA, see the "Rating Restrictions" section in CRS Report R42069, Private Health Insurance Market Reforms in the Affordable Care Act (ACA).

[46] As discussed in the text box "Calculation of the Premium Credit Amount" in this report, the actual credit amount will either be the premium of the exchange plan in which the tax filer is actually enrolled (Scenario "A"), or the amount derived from the formula based on the second-lowest-cost silver plan (Scenario "B"). Given this requirement, the examples included in this report assume that the hypothetical individuals/families enroll in the reference plan, even though credit recipients are allowed to enroll in any metal tier plan.

[47] Although person C is responsible for paying the entire premium, the premium contribution equals approximately 4.9% of income. This contrasts with person D, who has the same income level as person C, but whose premium contribution equals the maximum 9.56% of income.

[48] Revenue Procedure 2014-61 indicates that the dollar limits indicated in Table 5 of this report still apply in 2015. See IRS Rev. Proc. 2014-61, http://www.irs.gov/pub/irs-drop/rp-14-61.pdf.

[49] See IRS Notice 2015-9, http://www.irs.gov/pub/irs-drop/n-15-09.pdf.

[50] This penalty was in effect prior to the ACA. See IRC §6651(a)(2).

[51] This penalty was in effect prior to the ACA. See IRC §6654(a).

[52] For information about the individual mandate, see CRS Report R41331, Individual Mandate Under ACA.

[53] The plan selection count does not consider payment of premiums; therefore, it is not equivalent to a final enrollment count. The data point referring to premium credit eligibility is based only on plan selections for which such information is available. Office of the Assistant Secretary for Planning and Evaluation, Appendix Table A1, "Health Insurance Marketplace 2015 Open Enrollment Period: March Enrollment Report," March 10, 2015, http://aspe.hhs.gov/health/reports/2015/MarketPlaceEnrollment/Mar2015/ib_2015mar_enrollment.pdf

[54] While the 2015 open enrollment period ended on February 15, HHS provided a one-week special enrollment period for individuals who experienced technical problems or long call center waits related to enrollment through healthcare.gov. Also, individuals who experience a qualifying life event may qualify for a special enrollment period.

[55] "CMS Announces Special Enrollment Period for Tax Season," February 20, 2015, http://www.cms.gov/Newsroom/MediaReleaseDatabase/Press-releases/2015-Press-releases-items/2015-02-20.html.

[56] U.S. Congressional Budget Office, "Insurance Coverage Provisions of the Affordable Care Act—CBO's March 2015 Baseline," March 2015, http://www.cbo.gov/sites/default/files/cbofiles/attachments/43900-2015-03-ACAtables.pdf.

[57] The ACA establishes different eligibility criteria for cost-sharing subsidies for certain American Indians and Alaska Natives. For more information, see CRS Report R41152, Indian Health Care: Impact of the Affordable Care Act (ACA).

[58] The cost-sharing limits established under this ACA provision uses existing limits applicable to high-deductible health plans (HDHPs) that may be paired with health savings accounts (HSAs). Therefore, the annual cost-sharing limits that apply to a given metal tier plan is based on the cost-sharing limits applicable to HSA-qualified HDHPs. See Internal Revenue Service, "Revenue Procedure 2014-30," http://www.irs.gov/pub/irs-drop/rp-14-30.pdf.

[59] Actuarial value (AV) is a summary measure of a plan's generosity, expressed as the percentage of medical expenses estimated to be paid by the insurer for a standard population and set of allowed charges. In other words, the higher the percentage, the lower the cost-sharing, on average. AV is not a measure of premiums or the benefits package. Two plans with the same AV may have different premiums and different sets of covered benefits.

[60] See 45 C.F.R. § 156.420.

[61] The ACA did not explicitly provide appropriations for the cost-sharing subsidies. The Administration is currently funding these subsidies through the financing mechanism used for the premium tax credits. The House of Representatives has filed a lawsuit challenging the Administration's action, arguing that the Administration lacks the authority to disburse the money for the subsidies that they are providing. See House of Representatives v. Burwell, No. 14-cv-01967, (D.D.C., filed Nov. 21, 2014), http://www.speaker.gov/sites/speaker.house.gov/files/HouseLitigation.pdf.

[62] For additional information about these submission and payment processes, see 45 C.F.R. §156.430.

[63] U.S. Congressional Budget Office, "Insurance Coverage Provisions of the Affordable Care Act—CBO's March 2015 Baseline," March 2015, http://www.cbo.gov/sites/default/files/cbofiles/attachments/43900-2015-03-ACAtables.pdf.

INDEX

D

E

F

G

H

R

S

T

U

V

W